CultureShock!
A Survival Guide to Customs and Etiquette

Sweden

Charlotte Rosen Svensson

Marshall Cavendish
Editions

This 5th edition published in 2009 by:
Marshall Cavendish Corporation
99 White Plains Road
Tarrytown NY 10591-9001
www.marshallcavendish.us

First published in 1996 by Times Editions Pte Ltd, reprinted 1996, 1997, 1998, 1999; 2nd edition published in 2000, reprinted 2000; 3rd edition published in 2003, reprinted 2003; 4th edition published in 2006.
© 2009 Marshall Cavendish International (Asia) Private Limited
All rights reserved

The publisher makes no representation or warranties with respect to the contents of this book, and specifically disclaims any implied warranties or merchantability or fitness for any particular purpose, and shall in no events be liable for any loss of profit or any other commercial damage, including but not limited to special, incidental, consequential, or other damages.

Other Marshall Cavendish Offices:
Marshall Cavendish International (Asia) Pte Ltd. 1 New Industrial Road, Singapore 536196 ■ Marshall Cavendish Ltd. 5th Floor, 32-38 Saffron Hill, London EC1N 8FH, UK ■ Marshall Cavendish International (Thailand) Co Ltd. 253 Asoke, 12th Flr, Sukhumvit 21 Road, Klongtoey Nua, Wattana, Bangkok 10110, Thailand ■ Marshall Cavendish (Malaysia) Sdn Bhd, Times Subang, Lot 46, Subang Hi-Tech Industrial Park, Batu Tiga, 40000 Shah Alam, Selangor Darul Ehsan, Malaysia

Marshall Cavendish is a trademark of Times Publishing Limited

ISBN: 978-07614-5679-7

Please contact the publisher for the Library of Congress catalogue number

Printed in Singapore by Times Printers Pte Ltd

Photo Credits:
All black and white photos from the author except pages 26, 64–65 (alt.TYPE/ REUTERS); pages ix, 3, 4, 33, 37, 39, 54–55, 70, 94, 104–105, 109, 110, 111, 113, 115, 116, 118, 120, 127, 131, 134, 149, 160–161, 167, 170, 171, 175, 177, 188, 195, 203, 215, 221, 233, 234, 251, 252, 255 (Photolibrary). All colour images from Photolibrary except b–c (Getty Images). ■ Cover photo: Photolibrary

All illustrations by TRIGG

ABOUT THE SERIES

Culture shock is a state of disorientation that can come over anyone who has been thrust into unknown surroundings, away from one's comfort zone. *CultureShock!* is a series of trusted and reputed guides which has, for decades, been helping expatriates and long-term visitors to cushion the impact of culture shock whenever they move to a new country.

Written by people who have lived in the country and experienced culture shock themselves, the authors share all the information necessary for anyone to cope with these feelings of disorientation more effectively. The guides are written in a style that is easy to read and covers a range of topics that will arm readers with enough advice, hints and tips to make their lives as normal as possible again.

Each book is structured in the same manner. It begins with the first impressions that visitors will have of that city or country. To understand a culture, one must first understand the people—where they came from, who they are, the values and traditions they live by, as well as their customs and etiquette. This is covered in the first half of the book.

Then on with the practical aspects—how to settle in with the greatest of ease. Authors walk readers through topics such as how to find accommodation, get the utilities and telecommunications up and running, enrol the children in school and keep in the pink of health. But that's not all. Once the essentials are out of the way, venture out and try the food, enjoy more of the culture and travel to other areas. Then be immersed in the language of the country before discovering more about the business side of things.

To round off, snippets of basic information are offered before readers are 'tested' on customs and etiquette of the country. Useful words and phrases, a comprehensive resource guide and list of books for further research are also included for easy reference.

CONTENTS

INTRODUCTION

A book about Sweden—it ought to be easy to categorise the ups and downs of Swedish living, culture, language and people. After all, it is a very small country with only 9 million people, and is one of the most homogeneous populations in the world. Swedes are tall, blonde and blue-eyed, and their country is very cold and snowy, with polar bears and reindeer. Everyone skis and plays ice hockey, and is a pacifist, not liking confrontation. Of course it is one of the sexiest nations on earth, as everyone knows from tales of Swedish models and au pairs, and morals are a little looser. Other facts about Sweden that 'everyone' knows are how expensive everything is there, how left-wing Swedish politics are, that Sweden welcomes political refugees and contributes greatly to international aid, that Swedish food is bland and boring and that Swedish culture is a mix of depressing, deep hidden meaning type films à la Bergman and light bouncy pop music like Abba's and The Cardigans'.

But the reality, as always, is different. Describing and learning about Sweden is much more complicated than the image of blondes from a cold country would imply! In this book, you will find lots of information on the myths and realities of Swedish people, politics, geography, culture and everyday living. I hope that it will be helpful to anyone planning to move to or travel within Sweden, or to anyone who just needs to know more about the country.

You will learn about the dark-haired, dark-eyed Swedes, the indigenous Sami people and the many immigrants who have settled in Sweden. You will read about the long sunny beaches in the south, the rocky coastline on the west coast and the great forests and long winters in the country's north. No, there are no polar bears anywhere in Sweden, but the wildlife is varied and there are still large areas of unspoiled habitat and wilderness in Sweden, unlike most of the rest of Europe.

Not everyone skis; football is very popular and Sweden has qualified for most World Football Championships. Swedes surf, golf, swim, run and, of course, play tennis. In fact they enjoy the same sports as most other Western nations and excel in many of them. It is true that Swedes are proud of their neutral status and most avoid confrontation. However, they are also proud of their bloodthirsty warrior history and of the Viking times, and volunteer for United Nations armed forces around the world. Many Swedes are sexy. Many Swedes are not. Some have looser morals and some very strict, although it is true that certain behaviour considered immoral in other countries—such as living together without being married and divorce—is acceptable in Sweden.

And so on. There is much which is homogenous in Sweden compared with, for example, the United States, but there is still a wealth of diversity which is what makes Sweden such a fascinating place to visit and a very pleasant place to live.

WHAT MAKES SWEDEN SWEDISH?

The answer is, naturally, everything about it. This book will take you through the areas beginning with the geography of the country. It's difficult to really understand a country without knowing more about its background and politics, so you will find out about Swedish history and politics, especially its famed 'Middle Way', between capitalism and communism which, for years, was considered to have struck the balance. We will also look at the issues which have emerged in recent times with the Swedish way.

The Swedes themselves make Sweden what it is, and so there is a chapter about the people, including their ideals and ideas, as well as male-female relations and the class structure, followed by one on how best to settle in, with information about the details of everyday life, from housing to education. We also take a look at shopping, food, Swedish holidays, leisure activities and the arts—all vital to learning about the country.

When moving to Sweden, perhaps the best advice anyone can give you is to learn the language as well as you can. Yes, most Swedes speak English, but understandably prefer Swedish, and you will miss out on a lot of the pleasures of Swedish life if you cannot understand the language. Chapter Eight will help you find the best ways to learn and important things to know about the language. And finally, there is a chapter on what you need to know in business life in Sweden.

Learning about Sweden before you move, or in the early days of your life there, will make your stay there less frustrating in the beginning and ultimately much more rewarding. As the Swedes say, *lycka till*! (Good luck, said much more often in Swedish than in English.)

Perhaps the most distinctive feature of Sweden is how unspoilt it is in comparison with other European countries. More than half the land is forest and less than one-tenth of it is cultivated. That which is cultivated has relatively few people settled on it; 9 million inhabitants in 450,000 km of land makes for an average of about 20 inhabitants per square kilometre. However, when you're in the heart of Stockholm, it certainly feels more crowded than that!

ACKNOWLEDGEMENTS

My sincere thanks to Monica Rabe for letting me use her book *Living and Working in Sweden* (published by Tre Böcker Förlag AB, Göteborg Sweden in 1994) as a source of reference when writing *CultureShock! Sweden*.

Living and Working in Sweden has been invaluable help to me, in particular when writing the following chapters and sections:

- From Vikings to the Swedish Model
- The Swedish People
- Business in Sweden

For specific help with this book, I would like to thank Robert Grahm, who contributed photographs at very short notice. Britt and Dennis Eliasson, Malin and Bengt Johansson, and Anette and Peder Bengtsson kindly let me have photographs directly out of their own albums, for which I am very grateful.

Both Elly and Roland Svensson helped immensely with telephone advice, fact-checking and conversations about Swedish customs and culture, while Patrick Schyum offered advice and help on the various food sections, and with talking about Swedish customs in general.

Thanks also to my parents and to Catherine Neil for constant encouragement, and to Bengt, for reading and commenting on the manuscript, as well as being the 'in-house expert'—it would have been impossible without his help.

When I moved to Sweden I was often daunted by the differences I encountered—and this after living in several different countries! Many of my Swedish partner's friends made me feel very welcome and introduced me to a Sweden I grew slowly to enjoy and appreciate greatly. Especial thanks for this to Annika and Göran Johansson, Erika Biesse and Lars Wessman and Kate Parr-Grahm and Robert Grahm.

Finally, many Swedish and non-Swedish friends helped with countless discussions of culture, and with sending me articles about anything conceivably of interest for the book. All of this assistance and support has been greatly appreciated.

DEDICATION

To my parents, Neville and Catherine,
who took me to Sweden the first time.
To Elly and Roland
who made me so welcome when I moved to Sweden.
To Siobhán, Donna and Jenny,
who eased my culture shock.
And to Bengt,
the reason I moved and wanted to learn about Sweden.

MAP OF SWEDEN

Sweden occupies the eastern and largest sector of the Scandinavian Peninsula. Its northernmost region, Norrland, lies partly within the Arctic Circle.

FIRST IMPRESSIONS

CHAPTER 1

' "What do you think of Sweden so far?"
"There are a lot of trees." '
—exchange between author and her nine-year-old
houseguest, Adam Cattermole, from England

MY FIRST IMPRESSIONS OF SWEDEN came from my parents, who lived in Sweden with me and my sister in the late 1960s. They were temporary residents from Britain, living in Växjö, speaking no Swedish, and on a medical contract. My father's memory is of the advanced expectations of health care and the absolute politeness everywhere. He often said admiringly, "Sweden was the first country where GPs couldn't tell the socio-economic background of a child through a medical examination." My mother, who was at home with us, had a different memory. She remembers the formality of everyone she met and the fact that so many of their peers had household help. She says, "It wasn't that people were unfriendly, but they weren't friendly either." They both remembered the beauty of the countryside and the lovely cakes and buns!

Against this background, and a vague knowledge of Sweden's success in having gone a third way in the global political stakes (neutrality and social democracy), I moved to Sweden in the early 1990s to be with my husband. We lived in a flat in the centre of Göteborg (Gothenburg in English) and spent most of our time with other young couples without children. My impressions of the city were that there were a lot of blocks of flats and very little diversity of people. It was in the beginning of the first real recession Sweden had experienced in years and jobs were not easy to find. In addition, it felt a bit isolated from the rest of the world.

The beauty of the Swedish countryside extends into the towns and cities.

However, the countryside was beautiful, especially the forests and the coastline, and the Swedes I met through my husband were very welcoming and friendly. There were many things I loved about the country, such as the 'cosiness' of the cafés (there is nothing like a steaming cup of coffee and a fresh cinnamon bun, eaten by candlelight in a pretty café, as dusk falls outside) and the atmosphere in general. I liked the feeling of equality amongst people and the fairer access to education.

The conviction of many Swedes that there is only one right way of doing things (which was not my way) was a challenge, and the language was very difficult. I kept feeling that if only I could crack the language I would feel at home. We moved away from Sweden after a few years. But we visited often, and returned recently with two children.

Sit back and relax with the family.

My new impressions, building on the old ones, are very different. Now we live in a house outside the city, and are in the middle of beautiful countryside. My knowledge of the language makes everything much smoother (although I am still far from fluent) and the combination of the school system, freedom for children and outdoor living seems to suit our children. But, of course, those are simply our personal circumstances. Sweden itself has changed. There is more multiculturalism here than before which, although it has brought with it some attendant problems, is very welcome. Since Sweden has joined the EU, the country seems more open to international ideas, and you can find many more familiar things in the shops. Thanks to the Internet, you can stay connected worldwide, which reduces the feeling of isolation. Thanks to budget airlines, you can travel more inexpensively around Sweden and really get to see the place. There is more geographical mobility in general amongst Swedes as well, and an energy in the business atmosphere.

All these combine to make Sweden an easier place for foreigners to live; the challenge for the country is how these changes will combine with the best of traditional Sweden. My first impressions have turned themselves inside out several times; the best advice I can give anyone planning to move to Sweden is to stay open-minded about developing your own impressions. Don't expect too many similarities with home but enjoy Sweden for what it is.

INTRODUCING SWEDEN

CHAPTER 2

'Sweden may surprise you. ... Some aspects of
Swedish society strike the visitor as quaintly archaic,
while in others it patently leads the world.'
—*Blue Guide: Sweden,* 1995

THE REGIONS OF SWEDEN

Traditionally, Sweden is divided into three regions. The northern half of the country, Norrland, is very sparsely populated with a mixture of Swedes and Sami, the native nomadic peoples who migrate throughout northern Scandinavia. The southern quarter—called Götaland because of the Götes who lived there—and the middle quarter—called Svealand because of the Sveas who lived there—have a mixture of densely populated cities and sparsely populated countryside, and a mixture too of Swedes and immigrants. In fact, the name Sverige ('Sweden' in Swedish) is taken from 'The Kingdom of the Sveas'—Svea-rike. *Rike*, of course, means 'kingdom'. In modern Swedish this developed into Sverige.

Norrland

Norrland is the biggest part of Sweden, but few Swedes live there. The winters are very long and the summers short. In fact, the official first day of summer is not until the middle of June while the last day is in the middle of August. Summer in Sweden is defined as a time when the average temperature is above 10°C (50°F). In the very far north, around Kiruna, the sun does not set for a month in the summer and does not rise for a month in the winter.

Norrland is also one of the last true wilderness areas in Europe, with two of the largest national parks, Abisko

The open expanses of northern Sweden are part of Europe's last wilderness.

and Sarek, protected from development. Norrland features Sweden's highest mountain, Kebnekaise, which stands 2,111 m (6,930 ft) tall and is part of the 1,000-km long and 100-km wide mountain range to the west which forms a natural border with Norway, which is also the neighbouring country to the north, while the Tårne River runs along the border with Finland. Sweden has no other borders as it is surrounded by the Baltic Sea and the North Sea on its eastern, southern and south-western sides.

Just a small part of Sweden is north of the Arctic Circle, but even there, the weather is mild during the summer because of the warming properties of the Gulf Stream. In the winter, northernmost Lappland (a part of Norrland) has more than 220 days of snow. As can be imagined, the farmers work short intensive seasons! Many of the best Swedish ski resorts are in Jämtland in southern Norrland, including Storlien, Duved and Åre, where World Cup skiing events have been held.

Svealand
Svealand is the heart of Sweden, including Stockholm, Uppsala and Värmland. Stockholm, with over a million people, is like a big city anywhere, with its fast-paced city

life and accompanying pleasures and frustrations. However, Värmland typifies rural Swedish life, with red farmhouses, forests and lakes. Many of the biggest lakes in Sweden and parts of the very largest, Vänern and Vättern, are in Svealand, as are some popular ski resorts such as Sälen and Idre. The mountains aren't as high as in Norrland, but they are still beautiful and much more accessible.

Götaland

The southern part of Sweden was originally Denmark in Viking times, and there are still some accents and customs which are similar to Danish ones. The landscape tends to be flatter and warmer, with small lakes and hills instead of the great rivers and mountains of the north.

The second and third largest cities in Sweden, Göteborg (Gothenburg in English) and Malmö, are in the south. So too are the large glass-blowing region called Glasriket in Småland and the popular holiday islands of Gotland and Öland to the east. Although the way of living in Götaland is similar to that in northern Germany and Denmark, there are still expanses of unoccupied and uninhabited land because the population is so unevenly distributed. Nearly 25 per cent

Even the large Swedish cities have a feel of the open air about them. Here the harbour of Göteborg, Sweden's second largest city, combines waterside housing and pleasure boating with Scandinavia's largest working harbour.

of the population of Sweden lives in just the three largest cities, and most of the rest live in smaller cities such as the university town of Uppsala in Svealand and Vasterås, west of Stockholm.

Breaking the country up into three regions is the traditional Swedish division. However, there are two more ways of dividing up the country—into counties (*län*) and into municipalities (*kommuner*). Often Swedes will speak of coming from a specific county rather than from a city or an area, defining themselves, for example, as coming from Halland (on the south-west coast) or from Dalarna.

CLIMATE

Naturally, Sweden's climate varies greatly from north to south, but overall it is a temperate and cool climate. The coldest month of the year is January in the north and February in the south, and the warmest is July everywhere. The length of days is much shorter in winter and much longer in summer in Sweden than in most other countries because it is so far north, and that affects the temperature greatly as well. Another climatic difference is that the east coast tends to be drier and sunnier, while the west coast is wetter and windier.

BODIES OF WATER

The Swedes call the sea to the east the 'Inland Sea' because it is not very salty or rough, while the North Sea, which laps at the shores of the west coast, has more unsettled weather. The south-western coast has the waters of the Kattegat, the strip of water between Sweden and Denmark, to line its beaches, and has gentle seas. The sea has always affected Sweden greatly because it is so dependent on it, but in addition, there are also hundreds of lakes in Sweden.

FROM VIKINGS TO THE SWEDISH MODEL
The Viking Age

Perhaps the best known figures in Scandinavian history are the Vikings—bloodthirsty conquerors who spread across western Europe, Greenland, down to the Caspian Sea and

even to North America. Between AD 800–1050, the land that is now Sweden was ruled by different Viking chieftains in different areas. Although their reputation is one of warlike, violent men intent on conquest, their main aim was often trade and they had trade contacts as far away as India and China. As their trading grew more successful, they grew greedier and they went on to pillage many of the countries they had earlier traded with.

They had two main advantages over the peoples whose lands they ravaged. Firstly, they had developed ships which could be sailed or rowed, and were often small enough to be carried between rivers on land. The ships' flat bottoms meant they could sail very close to shore and yet the larger ships could carry up to 50 crew members with supplies to last for more than a month at sea. Secondly, death in battle was nothing to fear for a Viking. They believed that those who died in battle went to Valhalla, the Hall of the Gods, and gained eternal life. The Viking religion was polytheistic, with Odin the master of Valhalla, Thor the god of weather, Frej the fertility god and Balder the god of goodness and wisdom among the most important. Many of the old beliefs and stories are widely read today in collections of Norse mythology, both in Swedish and in English.

The Viking Legacy

Many of the Vikings who travelled overseas left their mark in the form of Nordic place names; many British town names have Scandinavian roots, and Normandy, in France, was known originally as the land of the Norrman, or men from the north. The Vikings who travelled west were mostly Danish and Norwegian; the Swedish Vikings concentrated on the east, and sailed the great Russian rivers down to Constantinople reaching as far as Baghdad and Bokhara to bring back riches. Called Rus by the local people, they gave the name of Ryssland, or Russia, to the area they travelled through, and left other names for cities along the way.

Their written language was that of runes, which they inscribed on stones when they documented battles and deaths, and also on arrowheads, jewellery and other goods. Many runestones are still found around Sweden, with the oldest, from around AD 200, in Gotland.

As more Vikings travelled in Christian lands, and brought back Christian slaves, more and more of them converted to the new religion. By 1008, the king, Olof Skötkonung, was baptised, and this marked the beginning of the end for the old religions and for the Viking Age.

Christianity and the Middle Ages

Olof Skötkonung united the two tribes of Sweden, the Sveas and the Götes, and the country became Christian by the middle of the 12th century, though many of the people held to the old beliefs of trolls, fairies and beings living in the woods. Parts of southern Sweden were still part of Denmark, and parts of western Finland today were then part of Sweden.

The Church became stronger and wealthier in the years to follow, and had a very powerful influence over people's lives. It also introduced the Latin alphabet into Sweden, as the Bible and other religious literature were all written in Latin. But the biggest change during the Middle Ages was the emergence of the state as an entity, raising taxes to build fortresses, buy land and equip the military.

The Swedish Viking history is that of a proud and fierce trading and warring people. This ancient monument tells the tale of Viking life; both battleships and traders are depicted. It is hard to reconcile such a bloodthirsty history with the peacefulness that is Sweden today.

The nobility built up power during the Middle Ages and divisions between the nobility, the Church and the peasant workers grew. By the end of the Middle Ages, four distinct classes had emerged: the nobility, the clergy, the merchants or burghers and the peasants.

During the 13th and 14th centuries, trade grew between Sweden and the Hanseatic League in Germany, and at the end of the 14th century a German duke, a distant relation to a former Swedish king, became king of Sweden. He was not popular with the Swedes, and Queen Margareta of Denmark and Norway (which was one country at the time) was asked to intervene to remove him. In 1389, she won a battle over the German-Swedish king and was declared regent of Sweden.

In 1397, the Kalmar Union between Denmark and Sweden was formed, and Erik of Pomerania, Margareta's great-nephew, was named king of Sweden. However, Margareta was still regent of Sweden and held the Union together with plans for a United Nordic Union which would act co-operatively. Unfortunately, after her death in 1412, King Erik concentrated more on expanding the Union, and waged many costly and unpopular wars against Germany.

The Swedish peasant leader Engelbrekt, from Dalarna, led a rebellion against this Danish domination in 1434. He was murdered and later honoured as a saint, but the Union had foundered by 1448 in a mire of disorder, civil unrest and fighting.

Gustav Vasa 1521–1611

In the early 16th century, the Danish King Christian II attempted to recreate the Union by force, but was defeated by Gustav Vasa, the leader who finally established Sweden as an independent power, which it has remained since 1523.

The story of how he came to power is a legend in Sweden. He survived the Danish murder of most of the Swedish nobility in Stockholm and fled to Dalarna to gain support from the peasants there. They were initially reluctant and he started off on skis to Norway, a fugitive from the powerful Danes. When the peasants changed their minds and decided to support him, they followed him on their skis, caught him up and told him they would fight with him.

The race through Dalarna, between Gustav Vasa and the peasants, is recreated every March with the Vasaloppet, an 90-km cross-country skiing competition with thousands of participants.

Gustav Vasa was elected king in 1523 and, as he needed money badly, set about breaking the power of the Catholic Church with the Reformation. He then became the head of state and Church, Sweden became a Protestant country, and the New Testament was published in Swedish in 1526. There were of course many other contributory factors to the break with Rome; Sweden had been affected by many of the winds of change blowing in Germany and the beliefs adopted were Lutheran, not Anglican.

In Catholic Småland, Nils Dacke led a rebellion against the new king but the rebellion was crushed by the military and ended with Dacke's death in 1543. Since Gustav Vasa's time, the Swedish crown has always been inherited rather than elected, although the current royal family does not trace its roots back further than the 19th century.

After Gustav Vasa's death in 1560, King Erik XIV inherited the throne. He is often called Sweden's Renaissance King, and spent much time rebuilding and adding to castles and encouraging arts and sciences. He was dethroned and imprisoned due to the constant power struggles in the royal family, and his brother Johan III succeeded him. Legend has it that Johan III poisoned his brother's pea soup, and that no member of the Swedish royal family has eaten pea soup since.

Johan's son Sigismund reigned after his death from 1592–1599, but Gustav Vasa's third son, Karl IX, ruled until his death in 1611. During these years, the power of the Hanseatic League was broken, Lutheranism was confirmed by the Uppsala Assembly of 1593, and Estonia became Swedish.

The Time of Great Power 1611–1718

In 1611, Gustav II Adolf, the 'Lion of the North,' succeeded to the throne and led Sweden into her imperial period. Napoleon considered this king to be the the equal of Hannibal, Alexander and Caesar on the battlefield. When Gustav II was drawn into the Thirty Years War (1618–1648), he won major victories. He was popular, particularly amongst the clergy, but his reign was a hard time for the peasants who had higher taxes to pay and also had to fight the wars. However, Gustav II Adolf also taxed the nobility heavily and expanded the power of Sweden greatly. By the time he died in battle in Lützen, Germany in 1632, Sweden had control over Finland and much of the Baltic states.

Queen Kristina, who succeeded her father, became queen at the age of six. She reigned until 1654, but abdicated the throne after converting to Catholicism, which was an outrage to a country which had fought so many wars against Catholic countries.

The end of Sweden's imperial age, or 'Great Power Time' as it is referred to in Sweden, came after the reign of Karl XII, who tried to force a peace with Russia and lost badly at the battle of Poltava in 1709. He was a legendary fighter but became very unpopular amongst the average Swede because of his constant and expensive warmongering. He was killed in Norway in 1718—shot in the head with a gold bullet, as it was rumoured an ordinary bullet would not kill him. Although when he came to power, Sweden had a great many provinces and much influence and when he died, Sweden had lost all the provinces except Finland and Pomerania, Karl XII is still revered by many right-wing and nationalist groups in Sweden, who mark 29 November, the date of his death, with marches every year.

The Time of Freedom 1718–1772

After 1721, the king lost political power and the country was ruled by the Riksdag, or parliament. Two parties, the Hats and the Caps, shared power for much of the century, until Gustav III took over in an absolutist coup in 1772. The country was in need of a strong leader, but Gustav III ruled as a dictator, which did not make him popular among the nobility.

The Gustavian Period 1772–1809

Nonetheless, the Gustavian Period was Sweden's Enlightenment, a time when the king brought French culture and philosophical ideas to his court. He established the Swedish Academy and a new interest grew in literature, theatre and opera. He ensured the reform of the Swedish language, so that it was purged of many foreign words, and the first Swedish dictionary was published. Religious freedom and a new interest in education for all grew during his reign. Various scientists, such as Carl von Linné (Linneaus, the botanist) and C W Scheele (the chemist), flourished during this time.

However, his manner of rule proved so unpopular that in 1792, he was assassinated, appropriately for him, while at the opera in fancy dress. A conspiracy of aristocrats had arranged it, and an officer named Anckarström carried it out.

At the beginning of the 19th century, Sweden lost Finland to Russia and traded Swedish Pomerania with Denmark for Norway. Gustav III's successor, Gustav IV Adolf, was deposed in an aristocratic coup in 1809 and replaced with his uncle. In the same year, the country adopted a new constitution which was maintained until 1975. It divided legislative powers between the king and the Riksdag (the Swedish Parliament), and created the post of *ombudsman* as a check on the powers of the bureaucracy. This paved the way for modern democracy in Sweden.

The Bernadottes 1810–1844

When the king died in 1814 without an heir, Sweden looked to France, to Marshal Jean-Baptiste Bernadotte, one of Napoleon's soldiers, to take the crown. He took the name Karl XIV Johan and, although he never learned Swedish, was a popular ruler until his death in 1844. He helped restore Swedish self respect after a long period of wars and unrest by establishing the policy of neutrality and working towards

Läckö Castle dates from the 12th century, but most of these walls are from the 17th. The division between nobility and peasants in Sweden was deep and the rise of a significant middle class did not occur until the 19th century.

Nordic co-operation. This began with the Peace Treaty of Kiel in 1814, which created a Swedish-Norwegian union which was to last until 1905. The current royal family is descended directly from the Bernadotte line.

Industrialisation and Emigration

Throughout the 19th century, the population increased dramatically, from 2.4 million in 1810, to 3.5 million in 1850 and 4.6 million in 1880. Swedes say this was due to 'peace, potatoes and vaccine', all of which had been unknown in Sweden previously. It was probably also partly to do with land reform, which took place in 1827 and gathered small parcels of land into more economic and efficient units. Agricultural output therefore went up, but the old social fabric began to disappear, scattering villagers to the cities and many abroad.

Reforms continued throughout the century, with *folkskolor* for universal education (for boys) set up in 1842, and a Riksdagsreform in 1866 which changed the parliament into a bicameral system and gave voting rights to all property owners. The Industrial Age came to Sweden in the 1870s with main industries in timber, iron and steel, textiles and glass.

The Swedish companies ASEA, Ericsson, SKF and AGA were all founded in this time and such inventors as John Ericsson (the rotary propeller) and Alfred Nobel (dynamite and later benefactor of the Nobel prizes) thrived. A new social class based on industrial workers began to grow, and by the end of the century, only 50 per cent of the population still earned their living through agriculture.

The Rise of Unionism

As industrial workers grew in number, they formed unions, and a number of other movements, such as the temperance and the women's movements gained popularity. All of these movements have influenced modern Sweden greatly, though it is perhaps the labour movement which was the most widespread. The year 1879 saw the first strike in Sundsvall and from then on workers joined unions to try and get better working conditions and pay for themselves and their colleagues. Many of the employers pursued union organisers and attempted to stop them by force, sometimes with support from the government. Often unionists were forced to emigrate in fear of their lives.

They were far from alone: more than one million Swedes emigrated, mostly to the United States, during the years 1850 to 1920. In the beginning this was often purely to escape the grinding poverty still prevalent in the countryside and the famine from several years of bad harvests in the 1850s. However, the Church of Sweden was still very strong and many wanted to have greater freedom of religion while others were escaping political problems. Conscription was introduced in 1901 to guard against Russian aggression and many men left Sweden to avoid military service. Emigration had the effect of depleting some villages, especially in Småland, and of setting up large Swedish settlements in the midwest of the United States.

The Early 20th Century

By 1900, 70 per cent of the population still lived in the country but the move to urban areas was increasing all the time. Unions were also gaining power and the political parties of the 20th century have their roots in these days. The Social Democrats were founded in 1889 and the Landsorganisation (LO), the biggest union, which today has over two million members, 90 per cent of whom are blue collar, was founded in 1898. As a countermeasure, the Swedish Employers Federation (SAF) was founded in 1902 but the momentum of the unions was growing and in 1909, there was a nationwide strike over proposed wage cuts. Meanwhile, all men over the age of 24 won the right to vote in 1909, and by 1921, women could also vote.

Since then, the country has been a modern, industrialised society, with democratic elections to the Riksdag which leads the nation. In 1920, the first Social Democratic regime was elected to power, with Hjalmar Branting as prime minister. It has always been the biggest party in the Riksdag since then and has held power for 70 years, with breaks in the 1920s, the 1970s and the 1990s when coalition governments were in power. (Coalition governments also ruled during World War II and briefly in the 1950s, but the prime minister in both of those governments was still a Social Democrat.)

Folkhem: The Welfare State

The Social Democrats began to set up a Folkhem, or 'People's Home' to ensure that Swedes would not have to suffer extreme poverty again, after the Great Depression of the 1930s. The Depression was felt keenly in Sweden, especially as demand for iron and timber, Sweden's biggest exports, fell away.

The Folkhem was built on the foundation of unemployment benefits in 1934, and rose steadily through the years with pensions for all in 1946, child benefit payments in 1947, health insurance for all in 1955, pensions with extra payment for workers in 1959, compulsory nine years of schooling in 1962 and parental leave in 1974. The ideal was to prevent problems, rather than cure them, and to eliminate poverty. After the insecurity and extreme poverty of the average Swede in the centuries before, the goal of creating an ideal environment for living was one that most Swedes were willing to support through high taxation. As a result, Sweden became the first country in the world where doctors could not tell the social class of a child by examining his or her physical health. The system worked so well that no matter what your profession, your child was guaranteed good medical care and you received special payments to ensure you could feed, clothe and shelter your family adequately. A complete welfare state is expensive to maintain, but as Sweden's economy and wealth continued to grow in the first half and middle of the 20th century, the problem of financing the social benefits did not arise until much later.

Neutrality and Peacemakers

Sweden stayed out of both World War I and World War II because of its policy of neutrality, maintained since 1814. In World War I, Norway and Denmark maintained a united front with Sweden and many Scandinavians volunteered as Red Cross workers. The war years were difficult for Sweden because of food and fuel shortages—a deciding factor in the election of the first Social Democratic government in 1920.

In 1939, the Finnish-Russian Winter War tested Swedish neutrality and 12,000 Swedish volunteers fought on the Finnish side. Many Finnish children were evacuated to Sweden during this war, and many stayed throughout World War II and then afterwards.

In World War II, Sweden stood alone as a neutral state after Denmark and Norway were invaded by German forces. This was a decision important to Swedes, who did not want to abandon their neutral principles, but it was a decision for which many Norwegians have yet to forgive Sweden. In the early war years, Sweden provided iron ore to the Nazis as a regular trading partner, as well as to the Allies. The infamous Transport Agreement of 1940, signed by Per Albin Hansson as a way of safeguarding Sweden against German invasion, allowed over 140,000 German troops to travel through Sweden enroute to occupied Norway and to Finland (after Finland allied itself with Germany against the Soviet Union). The Transport Agreement ended in 1943, to the relief of most Swedes.

Throughout the 20th century, Sweden has maintained its neutral stand and promoted international co-operation and aid through its financial, legal and personal contributions. The peacemakers after World War II include Count Folke Bernadotte, who agreed to mediate between the Jews and Arabs in Palestine for the Security Council of the United Nations, and was assassinated there in 1948. Another great figure was Dag Hammarskjöld, the second secretary general of the United Nations from 1953 to 1961. He, too, died while working for peace, though in his case death came in a plane crash in Africa while he was trying to resolve the crisis in the Congo. Both of these figures contributed to Sweden's international image as peace brokers, which Alfred

Unable to Stand By

Many Swedes could not stay uninvolved in the conflict on a non-military basis. One hero of the time was Raoul Wallenberg, the Swedish diplomat in Prague, who bent the rules to issue Swedish passports to Jews and other victims of the Nazis. Another was Count Folke Bernadotte, who received the official Nazi surrender from Himmler and negotiated the release of thousands of concentration camp prisoners in 1945. Bernadotte's white buses, as they were called, travelled up from Germany saving mostly Norwegian and Danish prisoners, but taking as many others as possible along the way.

Nobel had started in 1895 by establishing the Nobel Peace Prize.

The tradition of working internationally towards peace continued in the 1970s and 1980s with the work of Olof Palme as a negotiator in the Iran-Iraq war, and as a voice for the Third World. Even today, many Third World nations look to Sweden for aid and justice; Sweden is one of the most generous benefactors of aid to less fortunate countries, relative to size. In the 1990s, the amount of aid has decreased but the tradition of giving continues, as does the tradition of peacemakers. For example, former prime minister, Carl Bildt recently worked as a mediator in the war in the former Yugoslavia, whilst Dr Hans Blix's work as head of the United Nations Monitoring, Verification and Inspection Committee from 2000–2003 was well known in the run-up to the current war in Iraq.

SIDA

The Swedish International Development Agency (SIDA) is the Swedish organisation which distributes aid worldwide. The story goes that some nations think of Sweden as one of the world's superpowers because so much of their aid comes with the blue and yellow flag painted on it.

Neutrality and Militarism

Sweden's neutrality does not mean, however, that it has abandoned military training and spending. Quite the opposite; there is compulsory military service for all men and a large defence budget. Neutrality means that Sweden cannot rely on any other country to defend it because it belongs to no alliances. In spite of its peace-loving reputation, Sweden supports a thriving arms trade, partly because it could not afford to arm itself for defence otherwise. This double-edged sword of neutrality makes many Swedes uncomfortable, and there are many who protest against the arms trade.

Nevertheless, many perceive the arms build-up as a necessary evil and while, from the perspective of the current situation, an invasion of Sweden seems unlikely, a Soviet invasion was a very real fear during the Cold War. In 1981, a Soviet attack submarine was discovered stranded on rocks near a Swedish naval base south of Stockholm—

giving credence to the belief that the Soviet Union was a real threat.

Neutrality was a difficult issue during the referendum on joining the European Union (EU). Many Swedes thought that Sweden would compromise her neutrality by joining the Union, most of whose members had also signed the NATO alliance. This conflict is still current, with worries about Sweden having to contribute troops to an EU task force, which might enter conflicts that Sweden would have avoided. Sweden does volunteer troops to the United Nations Peacekeeping forces.

MODERN TIMES

After World War II, Sweden's economic strength grew and grew, and so did the welfare state. Growth meant that many immigrant workers were invited in to help swell the labour force and, through the influx of Italians, Greeks and Yugoslavians, Sweden became a little less insular culturally. With influence spreading from the United States through television, and with Sweden's traditional links with central Europe, the feeling was that Sweden would carve a middle way between capitalism and communism. Nobody wanted the social divisions inherent in pure capitalism, nor the oppression evident in communist countries. The aggression from both sides of the Iron Curtain turned peace-loving Swedes away.

The government continued to be Social Democratic, and Swedes built up their security and their way of life. It was hardly shaken until the oil crisis in the early 1970s caused unemployment, and events in the rest of the world, particularly the war in Vietnam, made Sweden sit up and take notice. In the late 1960s, Sweden stopped welcoming immigrants; the needed extra labour had overrun the available jobs. In the 1970s, the country learned to cope with high inflation and foreign debts. Partly as a response to this, there were wide ranging constitutional and educational reforms. By 1976, after several years of unease, the Social Democrats lost power for the first time in over 40 years, and various coalition governments ruled until 1982.

Another issue very much in Swedish minds was how to reduce dependence on the oil producing nations after the oil crisis of the 1970s. Much investment and trust was put into nuclear power.

By 1980, when a referendum was held, the effects of Three Mile Island and other nuclear power plant accidents had changed Swedish minds again, and it was agreed to phase the use of nuclear power out over 25 years.

Olof Palme

Olof Palme led the Social Democratic Party back into power in 1982. A very controversial figure in Swedish politics, he was prime minister from 1969–1976 and again from 1982–1986. His open condemnation of the American role in the Vietnam war earned him the disapproval of the United States (especially after he offered asylum to American draft dodgers) but his work for the United Nations in the Iran-Iraq war won him admiration. At home, he was seen as the left-wing champion of workers. He himself came from a wealthy upper class family and was a hero to those who thought of themselves as working class but a traitor to those who still liked to think of themselves as upper class.

On 28 February 1986, as he walked home from the cinema with his wife, an unknown assassin shot him dead. The whole of Sweden was rocked—their self perception as a safe nation, where the prime minister could walk unguarded in the streets of the capital was destroyed. Worse still, the assassin has never been caught. Twenty years on, Swedish police are still working on the case. Ingvar Carlsson succeeded Palme as prime minister, and vowed to continue his policies. In the late 1980s, however, Sweden was shaken further by scandals involving politicians, bank and company officials. The obedient nation who trusted in authority learned a degree of disillusionment. In the 1990s, this disillusionment only deepened with revelations about forced sterilisation of disabled citizens and possible wartime collaborations between the Nazis in Germany and leading industrialists and bankers in Sweden.

Swedes mark Olof Palme's death by placing roses on his grave. His murder is still unsolved.

Recession and the Welfare State

Not only was Sweden disillusioned, it was about to experience the worst recession since the 1930s. In 1990, prime minister Ingvar Carlsson pushed through various austerity measures, but by the 1991 election, the Social Democrats had lost power again, to a right-wing coalition led by Carl Bildt and the Conservative Party (Moderaterna). This administration, in power until 1994, set about dismantling many of the structures set up during decades of Social Democrat rule, by privatising state industries and cutting back further on centralised state power and benefits.

These cutbacks were inevitable; the full welfare state had grown too expensive for a nation struggling under the recession to fund. The economy worsened in the early 1990s, with unemployment reaching as high as 14 per cent and the currency taking a nose dive. By 1994, the country had voted the Social Democrats back into power, with Ingvar Carlsson back as prime minister.

But the country had changed both socially and politically, and the shift to the right has not disappeared.

Ingvar Carlsson resigned as prime minister on 28 February 1996, ten years to the day after Olaf Palme's assassination, when he first took office. His successor, Göran Persson, led the country through the 1998 and 2002 parliamentary elections, but the Social Democrats lost the 2006 elections to a coalition of centre-right political parties, led by Prime Minister Fredrik Reinfeldt. The economic downturn, which began in 2008, combined with a centre-right coalition government, has led to a re-evaluation of some aspects of the welfare system.

Split over EU Membership

Sweden joined the European Union on 1 January 1995, but only after a referendum which split the country nearly in half. Many of the just under 50 per cent who voted against this did so out of concern for diminished environmental and gender equality standards, and still campaign for Sweden to withdraw. The rotating presidency of the EU was Sweden's in 2001, and the then Prime Minister Göran Persson used it to draw more attention to such issues, as well as trying to get other European nations to adopt such Swedish laws as making television advertising to children illegal.

THE POLITICAL SYSTEM

Sweden is a constitutional monarchy. However, since the reforms of 1975, the monarch, although the head of state, has no political power at all. Until 1971, the parliament (Riksdag) was bicameral, but reforms in that year led to a unicameral legislature of 350 elected members.

In 1975, the constitution was revised for the first time in over 150 years. The foundations of the constitution are representative democracy, popular sovereignty and parliamentarianism. The Riksdag was decreased to 349 members to prevent tie votes. Elections are held every four years (until 1995 it was every three years) and places are won through a system of proportional democracy. A party must win at least 4 per cent of the nationwide vote or 12 per cent of a regional vote to be represented in the Riksdag. Every Swedish citizen aged 18 or over is eligible to vote; 90 per cent do. In addition, Sweden sends 19 representatives to the European Parliament.

Political Parties

There are seven major political parties in the Riksdag today; five parties polled less than 10 per cent of the vote in the 2006 election.

- Social Democrats: Socialdemokraterna
  The leading party which has its main support amongst the unions, and industrial and blue-collar workers. Their ideology is based on economic democracy, and equal distribution of wealth and power.
  (130 members after 2006 election.)
- Conservatives: Moderaterna
  The voters for the most right-wing party come mostly from high paid white-collar workers, and the so-called upper class. They share elements of their philosophy with the British Conservatives and American Republicans, advocating a market economy and a reduced public sector.
  (97 members after 2006 election.)
- Centre Party: Centern
  The former Agrarian Party's main voter base is among farmers. They favour free enterprise, decentralisation of power and an end to nuclear energy.
  (29 members after 2006 election.)
- Liberals: Folkpartiet
  The social-liberal ideology of this party includes advocacy of a guided market economy, with political democracy.
  (28 members after 2006 election.)
- Christian Democrats: Kristdemokraterna
  This party is broadly Christian-Conservative, and was a part of the coalition government in the early 1990s. Voters are attracted to it from across the spectrum, except from the socialist parties.
  (24 members after 2006 election.)
- Left Party: Vänsterpartiet
  This party is the successor to the Communist Party, and changed its name in the early 1990s after the fall of many Communist regimes in Europe. It campaigns for a planned, socialist economy based on state ownership. Many of the voters are highly educated white-collar

workers, although the traditional voter base was the working class.

(22 members after 2006 election.)

- Green Party: Miljöpartiet de Gröna
  The Green Party is one of the youngest parties, founded in 1982, and attracts many young voters who see protection of the environment as one of the main issues facing Sweden today.
  (19 members after 2006 election.)

In addition, there are often initiatives and newer political groups being founded. For example the June List (Junilistan), which is a cross-party alliance campaigning against a European constitution and a 'United States of Europe', started in 2004 after Sweden voted against replacing their own currency with the euro. A more recent group is the Feminist Initiative (Feministisk Initiativ) which started in 2005 with the aim of bringing more feminist issues into mainstream politics.

The Ombudsman and Openness

An important Swedish contribution to the world has been the *ombudsman*, an official appointed by the government to investigate complaints against public authorities. This empowers citizens and guards against abuse of power by any officials or governmental bodies. There are many different levels of ombudsmen in Sweden, but the main ones are elected by the Riksdag. They cover complaints against the justice system (JO) and preside in cases of ethnic discrimination (DO) and children's rights (BO). There are, in fact, four ombudsmen for justice, one of whom acts as the head *ombudsman*. If you have been unfairly treated by a public authority, you should always begin by complaining to the authority itself. If you still feel the case is unresolved, contact the relevant *ombudsman*.

Another particular feature of Swedish political life is the principle of open government. While the government may keep certain documents secret if they are matters of national security, other documents must be available to the general public if requested. In practice, this means that you can request to see any records concerning you, and you must be allowed to see the records. However, Sweden's policy of openness is causing some problems with fellow members of the European Union (EU), who prefer to keep such documents secret in their own countries.

Fairness and Justice

The history of Sweden travels from a deeply divided and class ridden society with the vast majority of people scraping a living from the land, to a society committed to equality and a high standard of living for all. In recent years, economic recession and changes in society forced Swedes to reassess how they want to be governed, and what is important to them.

Today's Swede is still attached to the land, but lives a very modern life, with all the technological advances that make life comfortable. The country still adheres to neutrality and peacemaking, donating aid to Third World countries and welcoming refugees, but it worries about the cost of it all. A sense of fairness and justice still motivates the Swedish people, even if today, the interpretation of what is fair may vary amongst them.

SWEDEN TODAY

Today, Sweden is a nation that is still trying to tread the middle ground, while succeeding in the modern post-Cold War world. The principles of fairness and equality are not lightly brushed aside from the Swedish psyche, but the cost of maintaining the cradle-to-grave welfare system is proving too high. Whilst remaining neutral, Sweden is co-operating with many non-neutral nations on defence issues, thus compromising its neutrality in the opinions of some.

Nevertheless, aspects of the welfare system are looked upon with envy by many other countries. In today's Sweden, although welfare benefits are being cut back, Swedes receive subsidised medical and dental care, housing benefit if needed, unemployment benefit if needed, free schooling, child benefit, over a year's paid parental leave, subsidised elderly care, subsidised childcare, free medical and dental treatment for children, and subsidies to help people who cannot work or support themselves.

For this, Swedes still pay very high taxes, though the extremely high levels famous in the 1960s and 1970s have fallen to levels similar to other European nations. Some people try to cheat the system by occasionally working black, or hiding their savings accounts abroad. The desire to get the better of the system is not new, but perhaps the disillusionment behind it originates only from the past 15 years.

Sweden faces many changes in society, and such challenges as the rising rate of crime and violence, high unemployment rates, the new popularity of some right-wing nationalist groups and even homelessness have no proven methods of cure. Sweden has less experience with facing these challenges than some other nations.

However, the crime rate in Sweden is still low, and even a considerable increase will not reach the levels of many other Western nations. But other principles in Swedish life, such as strict freedom of speech and openness, mean that certain shifts are much more noticeable than in other nations. One example is of nationalist groups, who are allowed to recruit members and apply for the government grants available for associations. The groups are still a tiny minority and Swedes are divided as to whether the danger they pose is great enough to abandon principles of fairness established in better economic times.

RELIGION

In spite of celebrating all the religious holidays in the Christian year, and of their history of Christianity, few Swedes are religious any longer. Until recently, a Swede became a member of the Church of Sweden automatically on birth, going back to the days when the Church kept census records. If you didn't want to be a member, you could opt out, which would mean you could save 70 per cent of the Church tax which would otherwise be added to your local tax bill. Now, no one automatically becomes a member, but can opt to join the Church at the age of 18 if they like.

Although few initially opted out, the numbers leaving are gradually increasing. Nevertheless, almost 75 per cent of Swedes are still members of the Church of Sweden, even though very few are regular churchgoers. More will also go to the popular services, such as *julottan*, the early morning service on Christmas Day. Sweden today is more of a secular society than a spiritual one. However, over half of all babies are baptised, with a small family party afterwards, almost half of all weddings are celebrated in churches and most funerals take place either in a church or in a funeral home with a religious service. About a third of all 15-year-olds choose to be confirmed, and are prepared for this either through regular classes and attendance at a local church or confirmation camp. In addition, many churches run preschools which are often well attended.

Religious Morality

Many of the morals of the Church of Sweden have been incorporated into the Swedish psyche. The Lutheran doctrine, adopted under Gustav Vasa, preaches submission to the powers that be—and Swedes today are still very obedient to authority. It also endorses diligence in one's duties, another

One of the major churches in central Stockholm is Katarina Kyrka (Church of Catherine). Originally built in 1656–1695, the church was reconstructed in 1990 after it burned down and reopened to the public in 1995.

common practice amongst Swedes today. Slacking off or shirking one's duties is seen as sinful, and while Swedes today might not use the word 'sinful', the belief holds sway in their minds.

Some morals have inevitably been relaxed. It is no longer considered at all sinful to live together before marriage (or even without planning marriage), and more couples have children out of wedlock than married couples. It is not uncommon to have a wedding and baptism ceremony combined, or to have a daughter as flower girl at her parents' wedding. There is a story that this originated long before the current liberal climate and that in rural areas in the past, a couple was allowed to sleep together after their engagement. This meant that a combined wedding and baptism ceremony would not have been unusual even then.

Now, the Swedish attitude to marriage and living together is that they are similar commitments. When a Swedish couple does get engaged, they both receive a gold band, which they wear on the ring finger of their left hands. When they marry, the woman often receives a second gold band or a ring with a stone. Getting engaged is not a signal for planning a wedding—many wait five, ten or even 20 years before deciding to marry. In the past few years, however, marriage has gained in popularity, though living together is still very common.

Attitudes to homosexual and lesbian relationships are more liberal in Sweden than in many countries. Single sex couples can marry and adopt children, subject to the same application procedure as heterosexual couples. Unmarried single-sex partners enjoy the same legal rights as heterosexual couples (these are the same in any case for married and unmarried couples).

Religious Denominations

Although most Swedes are Lutherans, and religious education is taught as part of the school curriculum, there has been freedom of religion officially since 1951 and unofficially for several centuries before that. This means that all citizens are free to practice their religion, or to choose not to practise a religion at all. The largest non-Lutheran Christian group is that of the Pentecostal Movement, with approximately 84,000 members. Other religions amongst the ethnically Swedish population include around 150,000 Roman Catholics and around 18,000–20,000 Jews. The numbers of both of these groups were boosted during and immediately after World War II, but Catholics and Jews have been entitled to worship openly in Sweden since the 1780s and there are established communities of both. The largest congregations of both are in Stockholm, Göteborg and Malmö, and there are religious schools for both in Stockholm and Göteborg, and also a Jewish school in Malmö.

Because of immigration from other parts of the world there are also an estimated 350,000 Muslims, of whom about 50,000 are religiously active, as well as members of Orthodox Churches, Hindus, Buddhists and members of other Protestant denominations represented in Sweden. All religions other than the Church of Sweden, which is financed through the Church tax, can obtain state grants in proportion to their membership and activities.

LOVE OF NATURE

Ask a Swede what he or she loves about Sweden and the most common answer will be nature or the countryside. They love the land itself, not just the freedom, the language and their homes, but the wide open spaces, the lakes and seashores and great forests. Swedes love their country in a way that some other nationalities may not understand, and it's not unusual to hear them say, "Sverige är fantastiskt!" ('Sweden is fantastic'—an easy translation from English).

Even the national anthem celebrates the beauty of the land, with no mention of royal families and only a brief and vague reference to past and future glories, unlike most other national anthems. The melody comes from a Västmanland folk song, and the lyrics were written in the 19th century by Richard Dybeck.

Du gamla, du fria, du fjällhöga Nord
du tysta, du glädjerika sköna.

Jag hälsar dig, vänaste land uppå jord
din sol, din himmel, dina ängder gröna
din sol, din himmel, dina ängder gröna
Du tronar på minnen från fornstora dar
då ärat ditt namn flög över jorden.
Jag vet, att du är och du blir, vad du var
Ja, jag vill leva, jag vill dö i Norden
Ja, jag vill leva, jag vill dö i Norden

The anthem salutes the old, free and mountainous north, with its solitude and beauty; it salutes the best country on earth, especially its sun, sky and green fields; and finally, it salutes Sweden's glorious past. The end refrain expresses the desire of Swedes to live and die in the north.

FLYING THE FLAG

The Swedish flag is often to be seen flying in front of schools, town halls and private homes. There are 16 national flag days most years, with one extra every fourth year on election days, when all flags should be flown, and many local flag days when flags in just one city or county are flown. Families usually also fly the flags when they are celebrating a birthday or wedding or special day. Even Swedes who do not seem particularly nationalist love their flag, and at major sports events, Swedes will paint their faces and dress entirely in blue and yellow to support the Swedish team or athlete. The flag, a yellow cross on a blue field, is the symbol of Swedish freedom.

The writer August Strindberg felt that the national colours ought to be red and green, to symbolise the red paint on the traditional Swedish wooden house, on a background of green fields and trees, and it is true that you see this colour combination everywhere. One of the most beautiful aspects of Sweden, for both natives, immigrants and tourists alike, is the way one can be in unspoiled countryside so near to the cities. Although this is mostly because of the small population density, Sweden realised early how precious its countryside was, and protected a lot of its land in the form of national

Swedes are proud of their country and fly the national flag on special occasions.

parks and other protected areas. As much as 3.5 per cent of the country is protected in some way, and much of the rest of it is unspoilt and unpopulated.

ENVIRONMENTAL PROTECTION

There are five different ways of formally protecting land. The first, the national parks system, is perhaps the best known. Land in the parks is protected for both research and recreational purposes. The biggest parks are in the far north, and when three of them, Stora Sjöfallet, Sarek and Padjelanta, are put together, they form Europe's biggest wilderness, at 5,330 sq km (2,132 sq miles). Other parks include Abisko in the north, Skuluskogan, Sonfjället and Hamra in central Sweden and Gotska Sandön, Norra Kvill, Store Mosse and Blå Jungfrun in the south. There are 28 in total.

Nature reserves protect areas which are characteristic of Swedish nature, or have a strong meaning for it, while nature conservation areas are similar but smaller. Slightly different are Djurskyddsområde which protect areas for the animals which live there. These are most common for birds, seals and beavers. Finally, there are Naturminne, or nature reminders, formed in order to protect the knowledge of the land's nature, beauty or its remarkable quality.

In this way, Sweden is working to preserve its beautiful countryside for all to enjoy. Among the animals native to Sweden are wolves, foxes, reindeer, lemmings, bears, moose, lynx, grouse, golden eagles and many other northern birds and mammals. About 60 types of mammal, 230 types of bird, 160 types of fish and 18 types of reptiles, amphibians and related animals make their homes in Sweden.

The Green Movement

Swedes feel this way about nature overall, which explains why so many are environmentally conscious. They recognise the need to leave the land as undamaged as possible for their children and grandchildren to enjoy, and the government encourages environmentalism through support for recycling, responsible farming and careful labelling of consumer goods.

The Swede's love of nature is strong and many make the effort to protect the beautiful wildernesses of their country. .

Recycling and Reusing

You will notice some of these green initiatives right away, because of the prevalence of recycling. Swedes recycle cans and bottles in supermarkets and food shops, where special machines pay them back their deposit in return for the bottle or can. Similar in concept to the American 'bottle bill', the machines make it easier and more convenient to recycle. In most residential and business areas, you will see large tips for collecting newspapers and glass that does not carry a deposit on it, and small bins for batteries. You must dispose of certain liquids, such as oil and paint, by giving them in at petrol stations. Some parts of these are also recycled.

Perhaps because Swedes are only a few generations removed from a rural society, there is also a trend towards saving things (such as glass jars to be used as jam jars, for example), or selling them second-hand (often through the columns of the Sunday newspapers or online) or else donating them to churches or sports groups who will sell them in second-hand shops to raise money. They have a tendency to refurbish and repair possessions rather than simply buy new items—partly again because of their history, and partly because material possessions are not as cheap in Sweden as in some other Western countries.

Other environmental initiatives include encouraging consumers to choose less damaging detergents and cleaning materials, and to buy more goods, such as toilet rolls, paper and stationery, made from recycled items.

Farming Methods

The differences in Swedish agriculture because of the effects of environmentalism may not be immediately obvious to you, but you may like to know that Swedish farmers work to keep their farms as natural as possible. This means that when you buy a chicken in a shop, it may not look on the surface as large and succulent as the chicken you are used to, because Swedish chickens are not fed with artificial hormones to encourage growth.

You may notice the difference in the taste of milk—called 'Swedish milk from the open countryside'—because the cows are not kept cooped up and fed hormones. The cruel treatment of veal calves and of any other farm (or domestic animal) is illegal.

This doesn't mean that Sweden is a haven of environmentalism, and that there is no pollution or abuse of the countryside. What it does mean is that Sweden works to protect its natural assets, and that the need for environmental initiatives is widely accepted. In fact the milk sold at McDonald's in Sweden is organic. To buy organic food in Sweden look for the KRAV mark, which certifies the food. You can find out more about their certification process at:

http://www.krav.se.

THE SWEDISH PEOPLE

CHAPTER 3

THE ROAD TO RESPECTABILITY

'To live as simply as a peasant in the countryside,
in a little red cabin overlooking water—
this is the Swedish dream... No good Swede would
ever pass up a chance to pick berries.'
—Mona Pers, in *National Geographic*, August 1993

SWEDISH CHARACTERISTICS

According to Baedeker's guidebook, the Scandinavians 'tend to be quiet and unassuming, patient themselves and offended by impatience in others. Their honesty, hospitality and helpfulness are proverbial.' It is true that the general character of the Swedes is similar to that of the other Scandinavians, and is shaped by a common history, language roots, climate and geography. Swedes, however, are often seen as more cosmopolitan and industrious than the Norwegians, and quieter and more reserved than the Danes. Respectability and a quiet life are very important to most Swedes, even though many rebel against this in their youth. Swedes themselves often joke about this; as soon as you have acquired the trappings of respectability and being settled (a terraced house, two children, a dog and a red Volvo estate car), you are called a 'Real Svensson' and fit right in!

They joke also about the differences between them and other Scandinavians. For example, there was an advertisement on Swedish television for a lottery game called Viking Lotto, which shows the reactions of winners from Norway, Denmark, Finland and Sweden. The Norwegians are kitted out in bright jumpers and are on cross-country skis, singing loudly and happily. The Danes are out at a restaurant, celebrating lustily with food and drink, while the Finns are raucously shouting and chasing each other around a sauna with birch twigs. Meanwhile, the Swede who wins is sitting on the couch in his living room, surrounded by his family. As the winning numbers come on the television, he says in a moderately pleased voice, "Well, it looks like I won." His wife says, "Well done" and smiles to herself, and the family settles back to watching television. And when you have spent some time in Sweden, you can imagine this happening!

There are many ways to describe the character of the Swedes; some stem from history, others from the difficulty of living in a harsh climate and others from societal norms and expectations. It is important to remember that there will always be many exceptions to every description, but many Swedes will fit in to the descriptions.

Rural Roots

Until 1870, fewer than 10 per cent of the population lived in urban areas. This means that almost all Swedes have very recent roots in the countryside, and spend their holidays in small cottages (*stugor*) in the country near where they, their parents and/or their grandparents grew up. Many Swedes are interested in folk culture and environmentalism because of this connection but, perhaps more importantly, the average Swede possesses a quiet pragmatism gained from generations on the land. They respect their old traditions, even if many of them no longer live by them. It is a quality that manages to sit comfortably with the modern and sophisticated attitude that Swedes also possess because, perhaps, both of these attitudes are based on a love of simplicity and directness.

Modern and Efficient

This juxtaposition of sophistication and a love of the simple rural life stems from Swedish history. Although Swedes are traditionally rural, they are also traders going back to Viking times, and have been industrialists for the past 130 years.

They are often seen as harder, colder, more efficient and less relaxed when compared to their Scandinavian neighbours. One way in which they do not differ is in their belief in improving life through modernity.

Swedes enjoy using modern conveniences and pride themselves on having a modern and liberal outlook on life. They like to work efficiently and take time off when the work is done. Leaving work on time does not mean Swedes dislike work or don't work hard; they simply believe that there is a time and place for work, play and family life. In fact, work is very important to most Swedes and, in common with many other Western cultures, they often define themselves through their work.

Punctuality

Their efficiency extends to a fastidious desire for punctuality. If you are coming from the UK or the US, you might think you know what they mean; it's easy to get impatient with people from some cultures who are more laid back. But Swedes are more punctual than even the average Brit or American, and it extends beyond the workplace to their home life as well. Much at work and home is planned, organised and scheduled carefully, and it can throw the whole schedule off if something is delayed. They are sticklers for fairness, and as they would not keep you waiting, they are surprised if you keep them waiting—even if it is just for ten minutes. At first this may seem a little extreme to you, but when you realise that it is part of the Swedish respect for other people's time, you will probably want to adopt it yourself.

Spontaneity is not a high priority to a Swede and nor is improvising. This is partly due to the inherent cautiousness which stems from years of poverty (and perhaps a fear that they are not too far removed from it!) For foreigners who see Sweden as very wealthy, it seems extraordinary that Swedes can be so worried about being poor, but the wealth is too recently acquired to allow Swedes to be comfortable with it yet.

Punctuality and Business
Keeping someone waiting to intimidate them, as happens in many other cultures, does not work at all in Sweden. It only serves to make the Swede believe that you are extremely rude and probably very badly brought up. If kept waiting for too long, he or she may just arrange to reschedule with your secretary, defeating your whole purpose.

Attached to this desire for efficiency and modernity comes a materialism similar to American materialism. Swedes like their dishwashers, mobile phones, electric bread bakers and so on. Such conveniences as central heating, televisions and washing machines are taken for granted now and in fact, central heating and televisions are considered a necessary part of modern living by the government. While Swedes do not like to work overtime as a rule, money is relatively important to them (if only to pay for the extras) and money-consciousness is another common characteristic of Swedes.

Reserved and Quiet

The quiet Swede is a very common stereotype, and often a very valid one. Naturally you will meet many gregarious and talkative Swedes, but you are unlikely to have many problems getting a word in edgewise at a meeting or dinner party. Swedes sometimes say that every conversation lasts seven minutes; after that it peters out until a new one starts. Sometimes the new one begins immediately but often there is a companionable silence before the next one.

It is said in many countries that politics, religion and sex are no-go areas of conversation. In a way this is also true in Sweden (except perhaps sex, about which Swedes are less embarrassed than most). The weather, money and sports are very common topics. Politics is discussed but it is rare for anyone to openly discuss his or her own political inclination. Swedes are not very good at small talk and prefer to get directly to the point, without being confrontational, of

The reserved Swede is happier socialising with a group of good friends. Here Swedes enjoy a meal outdoors, an activity they engage in whenever they have the opportunity. Silence at the dinner table does not make a Swede uncomfortable.

course. If it is impossible to be direct without a confrontation a Swede will often remain silent.

The expression 'silence implies consent' does not work at all in Sweden; in fact, it may be quite the opposite. A Swede may want to contradict you, but be too reserved or afraid of being rude to do so, and so remains quiet. On the other hand if he or she agrees with you, you will probably hear about it!

Åke Daun, an ethnologist at Stockholm University, wrote in a *National Geographic* article: 'Swedes are a painfully shy people. We're taught very early not to stand out from the crowd or risk making anyone uncomfortable.' He compares his own society to that of Japan in its emphasis on quiet conformity.

This comparison continues in the Swedish (and Japanese) dislike of showing their feelings. Although Swedes generally prefer to be straightforward, and believe that being open is very important, this does not extend necessarily to private or emotional issues. Swedes are often very isolated socially, with extended families living apart from one another. There is no pub or café tradition, no congregating in open areas and often, people do not even know their own neighbours. Instead, Swedes tend to socialise with friends from school, work, or sports or special interest organisations. However, their lives are often so full of activities, like work, holidays and home improvements, that most everyday social interaction usually centres around the nuclear family.

This can lead to loneliness for immigrants unless they adopt the Swedish way of life and get used to it. Indeed, it is very lonely for many Swedes—the high rate of suicide (15th among reporting nations) is sometimes linked to loneliness and to an inability or unwillingness to share emotional problems. It is also linked to the long winters, and to the higher rate of reporting suicide in Sweden than in other countries, so it's important not to read too much into the social isolation aspect of this type of statistic.

Service Equals Subservience

One way in which Swedes are not at all like the Japanese is in their attitude towards service. While the Japanese are very service-minded, in Sweden this is seen as almost subservient as well as superficial and, as all Swedes are meant to be equal, this makes them uncomfortable. Swedish shop workers, waiters and salespeople are often very friendly and can be helpful, but you will not often see the same standard of service as in Japan or the United States. (On the other hand, Brits will feel right at home.)

Direct Talking

Swedes have also been called rude and abrupt by foreigners used to different ways. This can be partly attributed to differences in the language but also, again, to the Swedish preference for directness and efficiency. A Swede does not want to use two words when one would suffice. Not only is it a waste of time and energy, but they think of it as purely superficial as well.

For example, buying a newspaper in Sweden requires perhaps six words: "*Jag tar den här.*" ('I'll take this.'), waving the paper, followed by *"Trettio."* ('Thirty.') and then by *"Tack."* ('Thank you.'), the last of which is optional.

If you have to actually ask for the paper, it takes even fewer words—simply say the name of the paper and hand over the money (a Swede will probably already know the cost anyhow). To buy a newspaper in England, on the other hand, can drive a Swede to absolute distraction. Start by asking for the paper, please. The newsagent will reply with the price, please. Hand over the money with a thank you. He or she hands back the change and the paper with another thank you. Take the change and the paper with a third thank you and goodbye. The newsagent says goodbye as well. This means at least nine extra words as far as a Swede is concerned—just think of the waste, and no one benefits from this! Better just to do the job and get on with it.

Opposite Opinions

This desire for direct speech and as little of it as possible led to frustrations between the Swedish and French workers who held meetings in the early 1990s when Volvo and Renault considered a merger. The Swedish workers complained that the meetings took far too long on preliminaries and formalities, and that once they got down to business they couldn't get a word in because the French dominated the conversation. As Swedes abhor interrupting, they waited for the natural pause in the conversation. Not surprisingly, it never came. (There were, no doubt, frustrations of an opposite nature amongst the French along the lines of, "They never contribute, we do it all!")

Seriousness

Swedes take life seriously. They work hard and are generally loyal to their job and to their company, and they take pride in the work they do. A refreshing difference between Sweden and many other countries is that there is respect for work across the spectrum of jobs; from a factory worker to a teacher, or a bus driver to a doctor, Swedes take pride in their work and strive to do well.

Honest and Reliable

It is impossible to say that a national characteristic of one country is to be more honest or reliable than another but

Swedes do take the concept of being 'fair' very seriously, and honesty is considered an important part of this. So too is reliability—it is not fair to go back on your word or to agree to do something and not do it.

Honesty and reliability are important parts of speaking directly and being open about things (except, of course, private or emotional things). The idea of 'saving face', common in many Asian countries, is not as common in Sweden. On the other hand, a Swede will rarely think or reason aloud, as an American might. Swedes will either answer directly or else keep quiet until it's all clear in their own minds and then answer directly. The time delay in answering can seem like prevarication, but it's more likely to be Swedish caution. It wouldn't do to go back on what has been said, so it had better be correct the first time.

A Dry Sense of Humour

Because of their reserve and lack of open emotion, Swedes are often considered to be humourless and inhibited socially. Another Scandinavian joke (told by the Swedes on themselves) is that of two Danes, Norwegians, Finns and Swedes stranded on four separate islands. By the time they are all rescued, the Danes have set up a co-operative, the Norwegians are out fishing, the Finns have cut down all the trees and the Swedes are still waiting to be introduced.

Fortunately this is a slight exaggeration! Swedes are not generally this inhibited and, although a bit of alcohol helps them relax (and the young sometimes rely on this heavily), they will generally be comfortable with people they haven't met before quicker than you think. It is not unusual for Swedes who are giving a party to either start the party with a game to break the ice, or else to have a seating plan at a dinner party to force people to speak with people they don't know. "We know ourselves," one Swede told me, "and otherwise we would only talk with the people we came with or have known for years."

They share a similar sense of humour to the British, in common with their reserve, and a lot of British comedy

programmes and comedians travel easily to Sweden. Such programmes as *Fawlty Towers* (a British production with John Cleese) are as well loved in Sweden as they are in the UK, and many Swedish comedians and programmes follow the same vein of very dry humour.

It is said that Swedes find it hard to laugh at themselves. You may think this peculiar, judging by the jokes they tell about themselves. The truth is probably more that they can poke fun at themselves but they do not find it at all amusing if a foreigner does. This is common with most nations, but one difference is that Swedes really believe that there is a right way to do things, and they have found it. Therefore no foreigner ought to laugh about it, even misguidedly, as a Swede would assume.

Smugness

This leads to one of the charges often levelled at Swedes. They are smug, always believing their way is better and therefore they are better. Many Swedes travel abroad for their holidays, and because there is so much foreign news and travel programmes on television, this leads Swedes to believe they are better informed about the lower standards of living in other nations, and confirms their superiority. Then again, they are far from being the only people convinced of their own superiority.

Ironic Agreement

Peter Watcyn-Jones, a Brit who lived and taught in Sweden for many years, sums up the Swedish character in his English teaching book, *What Next?* by describing a Swede as 'usually punctual, honest, reliable, clean, has his own teeth and is law-abiding.' In addition, 'he is shy, reserved, serious, industrious and finds it hard to laugh at himself.' Watcyn-Jones intended his essay to be used while teaching Swedes English, and it is meant to be ironic, but many of my Swedish students agreed with all he had said about them—it hit the mark!

SEPARATION OF AGE GROUPS

Although Sweden is a very homogenous group by nature, one way it has kept itself homogenous, possibly unwittingly, is through socialisation of different age groups. We can divide the population into six rough age groups, which follow their own paths, with little interaction between them and other age groups.

Small Children

Children up to the age of six are not in full-time schooling, but most go to a day care setting, either a preschool or a child minder. Since the vast majority of Swedish parents work, few children are at home with their parents after the age of 18 months, unless they have a younger sibling. Even then, many children will go to preschool for a few hours a day; it is considered beneficial for the children to learn to socialise and make friends.

School Children

From the age of six or seven, for at least nine years, children are in full-time compulsory schooling. After school, many go to special activities, ranging from sports teams and scouts to piano lessons and extra language coaching. Those whose parents work full-time often stay at the school afterwards or attend an afterschool centre, where they

Swedish children are encouraged to become independent younger than in many other countries. These Swedish children have come alone to a neighbourhood hill to sled on the early winter snow.

can play and be looked after by trained carers until their parents come to fetch them after work. Children gain early independence from their parents and the emphasis for them is on fitting in with their peer groups, rather than with their families.

Young Adults

Although children can leave school after nine years (generally aged 16), over 95 per cent of students stay on for the two to three years of senior secondary school (*gymnasium*) to gain further qualifications, either vocational or in preparation for higher education. It is not unusual for teenagers to move away from home and live alone in flats from the age of 18 and, as not all schools offer all programmes or subjects, many students commute to other towns to study, or for athletic training. Again, at this age, the peer group is very important, although not as many Swedes share an apartment with friends as in Anglophone cultures.

Parental supervision and involvement are not as important here as in many other countries. Teenagers must consider

Young adults are an important consumer group in Sweden, being at a stage in their lives where they have money to spend and little family responsibility. On average, women have their first child at 29 and men at 31.

what kind of work they would like to do from the age of about 14 or 15, because that will influence what subjects they apply to study at senior secondary school, and whether or not they will continue to higher education. When students are at university, it is very rare for them to live at home, and most receive student loans to enable them to rent flats, while many also take part-time jobs to help finance themselves. University students tend to be older than those in other countries; they often do not start until they are 20 or older and finish in their late 20s. All Swedish men between 18 and 24 must register for military training, but not all will be required to do the training, and this training can be delayed for study or work reasons. A popular option for many is to travel extensively, perhaps around the world or in Africa, or to work or study abroad, often as an au pair to improve language skills, or as a volunteer in a developing country.

Young adults are an important consumer group in Sweden; they often have good salaries and little family responsibility. The average age at which Swedes have a first child is 29 for women and 31 for men, and moving in with a partner (through marriage or not) does not entail the same responsibility as in other countries, as it is assumed that both partners will continue to work. This is one of the most visible age groups, as they are the ones who have the time and money to frequent restaurants, bars and nightclubs.

Families (Couples with Children)

The majority of Swedes settle down and have 1.91 children (one of the highest averages in the European Union) and the years between the late 20s and the mid-40s are often dominated by family life. Between full-time jobs, childcare and keeping up their standard of living, this group has no extra time for restaurants and going out. Most socialising is done with other familes in homes. The focus is very much on the family and the home during these years.

The Middle-Aged Group

Middle-age can be anywhere from mid-40s to early 60s, and this group tends to have more money and time after their children have left home. Most of the top positions in Swedish firms are taken by people in this group. In recent years, which have been difficult economically, there have been complaints from the younger generations about this group, particularly those who were born in the 1940s called the *40-talisterna*.

These people benefited entirely from the welfare state built up after the War and, after a period of radicalism in their youth in the 1960s, have now become more conservative. This is not unusual, but what bothers some of the younger generation is that they are still benefiting from the Swedish system, while younger Swedes are unlikely to benefit as much throughout their lives from the welfare system. Some say that the *40-talisterna* are like the cork in a bottle—until they move out of the way by retiring, the younger generation has no chance of moving up.

Pensioners

The age of retirement in Sweden is 65—although in recent years, many have taken early retirement as young as 58—but it is possible to go on working until the age of 70. As life

A presentation at a 60th birthday party. 'Even' birthdays are cause for celebration in Sweden. At 60, it's not time to retire yet, but even past the age of 70, many Swedes are helped to live in their own homes with dignity, by home assistance provided by the state.

expectancies are greater than in most countries (nearly 79 for men and 83 for women), Swedish pensioners have a long and often active life after retirement. It is not usual for older parents to live with their children and when they can no longer care for themselves, they live in either retirement homes or specially assisted housing for elderly people. If they can still live alone but need some assistance with shopping, cleaning and so on, the state provides help with this.

There is not very much daily interaction between the generations, and while some pensioners will help with babysitting, and some children will help care for their aged parents, for the most part they get together only on holidays and for family celebrations. This is similar to the situation in many Western countries, but the division is perhaps sharper in Sweden because the state has been so willing to step in and help.

IMPORTANT SWEDISH CONCEPTS
Lagom (Just Enough)

Two of the most important concepts in Swedish society are those of *lagom* and *trygghet*. Lagom means 'just enough' and stems from the days of the Vikings. They drank their mead from a common bowl, and it was understood that each man would drink *laget om*—not too little for his own sake but not too much so that all could share.

In a way, Swedes strive towards *lagom* because they strive towards moderation. One should work hard, but not too hard; eat enough, but not too much; have enough money, but not too much; and so on. This is part of the reason that so many Swedes have embraced socialist ideas, because they fit in with their ideas of fairness, equality and *lagom*. Certainly, the concept of *lagom* has made for a more harmonious society, but it has also had the effect of discouraging some Swedes to strive beyond 'just enough'.

The ideal of equality and *lagom* has, in the past, meant a taxation system designed to share the wealth more fairly and therefore evenly. This has sometimes meant that workers who earned overtime received very little extra money for it, and so people became more and more reluctant to work overtime, taking time off in lieu instead. In addition, a promotion with a salary increase was not worth very much financially because the worker would move automatically into a higher tax bracket. The desire for equality worked, at times, against the ideal of striving for more—the socialist policy often discouraged people from working harder.

Jantelagen (Down by Law)

Another discouragement comes through the concept of Jantelagen, or Jante Law. Swedes share with the Brits and the Australians a dislike for 'tall poppies' or high achievers, and the view that '*lagom* is best' accentuates this. While Australians talk of cutting down their tall poppies, Swedes talk about the Jante Law, which, although it is not the law of the land, counsels people to not boast or try to lift themselves above others.

Jante Law Translated

The Law, as translated by Monica Rabe, goes like this:

- You shall not believe that you are somebody.
- You shall not believe that you are as good as we are.
- You shall not believe that you are smarter than we are.
- You shall not think that you are better than we are.
- You shall not believe that you know more than we do.
- You shall not believe that you are superior to us.
- You shall not believe that you are good enough.
- You shall not laugh at us.
- You shall not believe that anyone cares about you.
- You shall not believe that you can teach us anything.

Many Swedes strive therefore to be much like all the others, to conform and fit in. If a Swede succeeds, he sets himself up for envy from his neighbours, friends and family—unless, of course, he succeeds just enough. This often has the effect of encouraging even the brightest students to settle for *lagom* jobs rather than more challenging options. To aim higher would mean that the student thought he

or she was better than others and worth more, so it isn't as acceptable. This affects the would-be entrepreneurs, risk takers, artists and inventors as well as the genuinely average student.

The educational system over the past 30 years has not tried to alter this, and has worked hard to instill the values of consensus and co-operation into children. Both of these very worthy ideals often make children see competition as a negative thing, and also see keeping a low profile as a good thing. Average is good, orderly is good. However, recent educational reforms are now working towards keeping egalitarian principles while still catering for and encouraging brighter students.

Lagom is in many ways an excellent concept, and fits in well with the Swedish ideas of fairness. It is likely that it will be more and more challenged as Sweden leaves behind some of its international isolation, and that Swedes, appreciating consensus as they do, will work to incorporate the good aspects of it into their new societal ideas. After all, there are still entrepreneurs, artists, inventors and high achievers in Sweden in spite of the Jante Law and *lagom*. And Swedes probably wish that more countries in the world would practice *lagom*. It would, after all, be fairer.

Trygghet (Safe and Secure)

Trygghet can be translated into security, or safety, and is a concept very dear to the Swedish heart. Swedes prefer to be cautious and attempt to foresee the risks before committing to a decision. In business, they often evaluate and document everything before making their minds up—it's always better to be on the safe side.

As mentioned before, this fits in with the Swedish love of planning and predictability, and also of consensus. In their view, it can't be a good decision if there is disagreement about it. If this sounds boring to you, remember that it also fits in with the quality of reliability—once a decision has been made a Swede will generally hold to it, and mean what he or she says.

Part of the ideal behind the People's Home welfare state started from the idea of *trygghet*. The welfare state provides safety from all things uncomfortable or unpleasant, allows Swedes to plan safely and helps ensure a tranquil life for all. Swedes feel more secure when they know exactly what is going to affect them, and this may also be why they speak directly and avoid too much subtlety in conversation.

This directness extends to the government; all documents are open for the public to examine, and you can always be granted access to documents about yourself (such as your health records, police records, etc.) This is important to the Swedish sense of security. It has also caused problems in the European Union recently, when some papers classed as private were released in Sweden, as they must be by law. They were not released into other EU nations, which do not have the same tradition, and there was much embarrassment and confusion over the resolution of the problem.

The Swedish love of safety is evident in the goods in the shops and in the consumer choices they make. The strong safety record of Volvo cars, the stringent factory regulations for worker safety and the plethora of smoke alarms, child safety seats, and other safety items on sale, all point towards it. Seat belts—in both the front and back seats—are required in cars in Sweden, and many medicines available over the

Films and television programmes are often censored for the viewers' sake. These same films are sometimes censored of their sex scenes in the United States. Sweden is comfortable with sex scenes but considers violence in films to be more dangerous than Americans do.

counter in the US and the UK are prescription only or not even for sale in Sweden.

Trygghet is not only freedom from danger and fear, but also a feeling which develops when a Swede feels secure in his or her job, home and family. For this reason, Swedes move around the country less often than Brits or Americans do, and would certainly be loath to move for work reasons, especially later in life. It is also why the recent economic uncertainty has hit Sweden so hard; Swedes have been so used to the *trygghet* of their jobs before the late 1980s that the rising unemployment level probably affected them more than it would have another nation.

THE CLASS SYSTEM

Sweden has worked hard to eradicate its class system over the past 70 years. The original four divisions of nobility, clergy, merchants and peasants began to disappear at the end of the 18th century and were long gone by the turn of the 20th century. The rise of the middle class gave way to the three-class system that exists today. The first, the upper class, includes the few people who have money, influence and power in Sweden. They may have inherited wealth or have acquired it themselves. The third class includes those who do not fit into society, such as criminals or drug addicts. This is also a small class. The middle class, with by far the vast majority of Swedes, includes everyone else. This means that the majority of Swedes have more or less equal status and, in turn, often more or less equal buying power.

As mentioned before, many of the professions in Sweden are accorded equal respect, and through the progressive taxation system, many workers receive similar pay packets each month, and both of these have contributed to the large middle class.

Another factor is the lack of infrastructure for an upper class. Unlike many other countries, there are very few private schools or clubs, and having servants, or even a weekly cleaner is not very common. Swedes expect to do their work for themselves, and the idea of asking someone else to do their dirty work for them is abhorrent. There is also an informality in everyday life which means that titles, such as Mr or Mrs (or Sir or Lady!) are rarely used, and that people prefer to use first names.

However, the past 15 years has seen a shift to the right and Sweden has seen a significant growth in the division between rich and poor. It remains one of the countries with the smallest such division in the world, nevertheless. Certainly this highlights some class differences again, but the society is so firmly egalitarian that it is hard to imagine it returning to the old ways again.

THE ROYAL FAMILY

One remnant of the old ways which still remains is the royal family. The present king, Carl XVI Gustaf, and his queen, Silvia, are popular enough to withstand any occasional talk of republicanism. The king is officially the head of state, but holds no political power. He succeeded his grandfather to the throne in 1973, when he was only 27, because his father had died when he was still a baby. In 1976, he married Silvia Renate Sommerlath, a half-German, half-Brazilian beauty who is liked by the Swedish people for her adoption of Swedish customs and language.

The crown princess, Victoria, who will accede to the throne after her father (in Sweden, the heir is the first-born child, not the first-born son), was born in 1977; her brother Carl Philip in 1979 and sister Madeleine in 1982. Crown Princess Victoria is engaged to marry Daniel Westling in 2010. The motto adopted by the king is *För Sverige i tiden* ('For Sweden with the times'), which is typical of the modern outlook of this monarch. His grandfather, who is often called 'The Old King'

The goal of abolishing the monarchy and being a republic was part of the former Social Democratic government's manifesto for years, but not of the current coalition government. In addition, it was never considered an important enough issue to drive through the government, as the royals are much respected and work hard to publicise Sweden abroad.

The Swedish Royal Family: (from left to right) King Carl XVI Gustaf, Princess Madeleine, Crown Princess Victoria, Prince Carl Philip and Queen Silvia.

because he reigned for so long and became so old, had the motto *Plikten framför allt* ('Duty above all').

MEN AND WOMEN

Sexual discrimination in Sweden is illegal. Over 80 per cent of Swedish women work outside the home and 47 per cent of the labour market is female. Women can be ordained priests in the Church of Sweden and the Equal Opportunity Act of 1980 ensures that employers must take active steps to promote equality in the workplace. Sweden has done a lot, particularly in recent years, to work towards equal rights for men and women.

FAMILY RELATIONS

Gender equality extends as well to family relations. For example, spouses are taxed separately so that there is no tax advantage either way. Because it is very common for men and women to live together without being married, a law, called *sambolagen*, was enacted to protect their rights. *Sambo* comes from *samboende*, or 'living together', and it is common to refer to a live-in partner as a *sambo*. *Sambo* law means that all belongings of a *sambo* couple are owned equally and must be divided equally if the couple separate. To get this kind of protection in most other countries, the couple would have to draw up a special contract; in Sweden, couples sometimes draw up their own contracts anyhow, but the law protects them if they do not.

Equality has been furthered also through sharing of childcare. Everyone is entitled to over a year's paid leave from work to care for a new baby, and that can be shared equally between the father and the mother if wished. Assisted childcare places, time off when a child is ill and state sponsored after-school homes all make it easier for women to advance professionally.

Swedish women still complain that men do not help out enough around the home, and that while they get help with childcare, they are responsible for it, not their male partners. In comparison with many other nations, however, Swedes are 'new men' indeed, and it is a rare one who will not share, at least partly, in housework or childcare.

Unfortunately, despite the initiatives, Swedish women still earn less on average than men, and many of them work part-time while their children are small. More men go into higher paid sectors, while women are concentrated in the health care, education and service sectors, which tend to be lower paid. This does not seem set to change in the near future. There are now more women studying at university level than men, but the majority of those studying technical or scientific subjects are still men. Because parental leave is paid at a percentage of one's salary, the majority of Swedish fathers take only three months or fewer, so that their pay is not affected while their lower paid partner takes often over a year's leave for childcare.

Of course, many women would prefer to stay at home for longer with their children, but few families can afford to maintain their lifestyles without two salaries. The 'superwoman' myth of being able to raise children (albeit with much help), have a demanding and successful career and still keep a beautiful house is as prevalent (and as impossible) in Sweden as it is in other cultures.

The battle for equality between men and women is an ongoing one, but has come much further in Sweden than in most other countries. This may take some getting used to for you, or you may herald it as a wonderful thing but you will certainly notice it.

THE SAMI

The Sami are the indigenous people of Scandinavia. According to Sametinget, there are approximately 80,000 Sami across the five northern countries, with about 20,000 in Sweden. (See http://www.eng.samer.se/ for more information.) In English, they are sometimes called Lapps, but the name they call themselves, and the preferred name, is Sami (Samerna in Swedish).

They are thought to have come to northern Scandinavia about 9,000 years ago, as nomads, and their way of life stayed the same for centuries, until recent years. They lived off hunting, trapping and fishing, and ate mostly reindeer, beaver and salmon. They also traded in furs and crafts, and were reindeer breeders, herding their reindeer across the north with little thought of borders. Their history and religion has very little in common with that of Sweden as a whole, and few would identify themselves as Swedish.

Their language is Finno-Ugric, and has nothing in common with Swedish, which is an Indo-European language with Germanic roots. There are three main branches of the language and nine dialects, and it reflects their way of life. For example, there are eight different words for the seasons, as they have the four that we do, plus four more in between those. They are also said to have hundreds of words for snow, and their language can describe an individual reindeer from amongst a herd of hundreds. In recent years, their written language and literature has begun to develop, and Sami children can go to Sami language preschools, and their culture and history is taught in schools which teach in both Swedish and the Sami language.

In the past century, problems have arisen for the Sami because the lands they inhabit and use for their herding and hunting have been found to harbour great mineral wealth. The great rivers of the north have often been dammed for hydroelectricity and the growth of the forestry industry has increased industrial interest in the north. Stricter national borders have sometimes made it more difficult for the Sami to cross to different parts of their land. Many younger Sami have given up the old ways of life and moved to Stockholm to live as modern Swedes.

Only about 10 per cent of Sami today are full time reindeer breeders and their methods have changed markedly. They use snowmobiles, mobile phones and helicopters to help in their work, although they prefer to live otherwise as they have always done. This, ironically, leads to some conflict with the burgeoning tourist trade in the region, who want to see picturesque scenes of old Sami customs without the modern trappings.

To help combat these problems, the Nordic Sami Council was formed in 1986, and a flag created for the Sami people.

The Sami who live in Sweden have had their own parliament since 1993. Unfortunately, the Sami were forced to take this development with a grain of salt; on 25 August 1993, the day before the parliament was formed, the Swedish government abolished hunting restrictions for non-Sami in mountain regions. Many Sami felt that the government had given with one hand and taken with another. Trying to come to terms with the modern and the traditional is an ongoing issue in Sweden.

THE NEW SWEDES

After the great emigration in the last century, Sweden has seen much immigration this century, and many of these newest Swedes have settled into Sweden, changing the country slightly and assimilating themselves. About a million people in Sweden today are reckoned to be immigrants, but that includes anyone born to an immigrant, even if their other parent is Swedish and they themselves were born in Sweden. The majority of all immigrants come from other Nordic countries.

The first great wave started during the 1930s and 1940s, when Finnish children were evacuated during the Finnish-Russian Winter War and as many as 30,000 refugees from the Baltic countries sought shelter. Many also escaped the German occupation in Denmark and Norway to settle in Sweden.

After the World War II, Swedish industry was booming and had a shortage of workers. Representatives of Swedish companies recruited workers from many countries, and many came from Germany, Italy, Greece, Austria, Belgium and the former Yugoslavia. When they arrived in the 1950s and 1960s, they were welcomed—the labour was badly needed.

At that time, Sweden also welcomed many refugees. From 1950–1973, around 25,000 Eastern Europeans fled to Sweden, particularly from Hungary in 1956, Czechoslovakia in 1968, and Poland in the 1960s. From 1967–1974, about 10,000 Greeks were granted asylum in Sweden, as were around 800 Americans, who refused to fight in the Vietnam

The Sweden of today is home to many immigrants who have come to live in the country over the years.

War and applied to Sweden for asylum. Various international disasters and tragedies have led to an influx of people from different parts, including about 1,000 Ugandans in the 1970s, 12,000 Assyrians and Syrians in 1967 and beyond, 11,000 from Latin America, and 2,000 from Vietnam.

All of these refugees have been welcomed and were offered assistance for settling into Swedish life. In recent years, the refugees have come from Eritrea, Somalia, Ethiopia, Iran, Iraq, Turkey and the former Yugoslavia, but their welcome has not been so hearty. The government has cut down on the number of refugees Sweden can afford to accept, and there has been some anti-refugee, anti-immigrant feeling amongst some Swedes. The majority of Swedes are proud that they are able to share a safe haven with people in need, but sometimes they wonder how it is all to be financed. Remember that Swedes need a high level of security, and anything which might threaten that worries them. It is always easier for a nation to welcome immigrants and refugees when the economy is strong.

This worry about high levels of immigration in the past meant that in 1967, the government imposed immigration controls. The Nordic market remained, and remains, open, but it is increasingly difficult to immigrate to Sweden unless one has a family or business connection. Currently just over a million immigrants live in Sweden, of which about a third come from Europe (outside Scandinavia), just over a quarter come from other Nordic countries and most of the rest come from Asia (including Turkey). Although nearly 11 per cent of inhabitants are foreign-born, almost half of those have become Swedish citizens.

Swedish society prefers harmonious assimilation from its immigrants, and many immigrants do just that. There are many immigrant support groups both for specific nationalities and for immigrants in general which help people to keep their cultures intact while living as Swedes. All immigrants are protected by legislation against discrimination on the grounds of race, ethnicity or nationality. This legislation also says that immigrants have the right to equality, freedom of choice and co-operation from Swedes. After two years of living in Sweden, immigrants can vote in local elections.

Immigration from non-Nordic countries is very gradually changing the face of Sweden, and the newest Swedes are making a subtle and often much welcomed mark on the country, from their small businesses to their contributions to the national sports teams and the arts.

SOCIALISING WITH THE LOCALS

CHAPTER 4

'Lagom är bäst'
('Just enough is best')
—Swedish proverb

MAKING FRIENDS WITH THE SWEDES

As you'll have guessed from the previous chapter's description of Swedes, it isn't especially easy to make friends with them. Between their reserve, quietness and general contentment with the status quo, many seem happy to stick to the friends they have had for years. Add to this the general busy-ness of the average Swedish household and you may realise the challenge ahead of you.

Indeed, it may take awhile to socialise with the locals. Many Swedes are not friendlier than they need to be; and part of the trick of not being offended by this is realising that they are not being unfriendly by their standards. Of course, this does not mean Swedes you meet through mutual friends are likely to remain distant, but rather those you work with, whose children go to the same school as yours, who are your neighbours. Many is the story of the newcomers moving into a block of flats whose first encounter with the neighbours is the note on the door asking them to be quieter when they come in late at night, rather than a friendly 'welcome to the building!'. This is not to daunt you, but to help you develop realistic expectations.

Swedes tend to keep themselves to themselves, and it may take a while to be invited home to anyone. The Swedish media regularly publish articles on how immigrants complain they know no Swedes and have never been invited home to them. At the same time, Swedes take friendship seriously, and an invitation is not a casual affair. The American's lighthearted 'come over some time, we'll grab a pizza' is utterly confusing for a Swede who doesn't know if it's a real invitation or when he should come; and he may feel somewhat offended that the host does not intend to prepare a special meal for him. Because so many people are involved in complicated schedules (day care pickup, sports activities, combining work and study, dual career couples, dual custody families, etc), most people simply feel too busy to entertain very often. In addition, the very nature of Swedes does not lead to spontaneity and drop-in guests are not at all common, or particularly appreciated. The Swedes are often not accustomed to socialise during the week so that only leaves weekends; when, if they are home, they are tired.

Which leads us to a more recent custom in Sweden, that of the sacred *myskväll*, which means literally 'cosy evening'. Some cultural commentators have said that the new tradition of the Friday night cosy evening has taken on the importance for the family that church and Sunday lunch had two generations ago. It is nothing fancy; but on a Friday night, many families have a special meal that everyone likes and then they all relax with snacks and drinks in front of the TV and watch some rented DVDs. The children stay up late as it's a Friday, and everyone catches up on the week and makes plans for the weekend. One of the unwritten rules seems to be 'nobody but family included', although among the younger generation, it's more likely to be a close set of friends.

Although it starts to sound impossible to meet Swedes as friends, this is, of course, not the case. Just don't expect much friendliness from the average acquaintance. In fact, in the communal laundry room of many apartment buildings, count yourself lucky to avoid outright hostility. This isn't towards foreigners; everyone gets the same treatment. However, there are ways to get to know your neighbours, fellow parents and colleagues better.

One of the best is to volunteer for a committee or group job, such as being a class parent, or a sports group at work. If you live in a suburban neighbourhood, whatever you do, don't miss the annual 'clear up day' when everyone is up and about (usually a Saturday in spring), clearing up the communal walkways, play areas, etc. In some neighbourhoods, missing this can even incur a fine; even if it doesn't, it's a good way to meet other people.

Another way, of course, is to invite people over yourself. They will probably accept and have an enjoyable time. Just don't hold your breath waiting for a return invitation and don't take it personally if an invitation is a long time coming. Inviting people home isn't an integral part of Swedish culture—that is, not until they feel they know you really well.

ALTERNATIVE LIFESTYLES

Although Swedes often live quite similar lives, it is impossible to generalise about such a large number of people. There are people living alternative lifestyles just as in other countries, and there is the freedom to do so. People will bat an eyelid, and they may meet disapproval, especially from the older generation and in smaller communities, but rarely will they meet with censure. The more common reaction would be to shrug and say 'if they want to live that way, that's up to them'. There isn't a movement on the scale of the 1970s communal living movement (in fact, Sweden has a very high percentage of single person households); and in a country so governed by the Insurance Office and the Tax Office, it can take a lot of explaining if you wish to be 'out of the system'. Small victories which have been made by people wishing to live differently are those advocating the right to homeschool their children and the right to set up their own schools (subject to inspection).

Quite aside from alternative lifestyles, there are also many Swedes who have lived abroad, or who simply don't fit the mould of the average Swede. My personal experience has been one of luck in having bought a home in a neighbourhood with at least two such couples, who invited me over after only six months' acquaintance. You may well have similar luck with your neighbours or work colleagues. It is likely that a first invitation in either instance will be for a dinner party or a coffee/*fika* on an afternoon, although a second invitation is more likely to a larger party, perhaps during the Christmas season, for midsummer, or for a crayfish party in August.

THE INVITATION HOME
Dinner Parties

Swedes are not as open about inviting people home as many other nationalities, so don't worry if it takes a while before you get any invitations. It probably doesn't mean you are unpopular and eventually, when you know your colleagues or friends a bit better, you are likely to be invited over.

The invitations are usually verbal except for formal or special occasions. Sometimes a written invitation will have the letters 'OSA' and a telephone number at the bottom, which means you should ring to tell the hosts whether you will be able to attend or not. On the day of the party, it is important to be punctual. There are jokes about Swedes waiting on the doorstep for five minutes in order to be able to ring the doorbell at 7:00 pm promptly—and you may find that this actually happens in Sweden. In any case, if you are invited for 7:00 pm for a meal, the host or hostess will have planned for the food to be ready then or soon afterwards, so it would be rude to keep them waiting. The custom of 20 minutes late being polite is not practised in Sweden. Neither should you be early; but this is preferable to being late.

Most guests bring a small present for the host and hostess, such as chocolates, wine or flowers. If it is your first time at someone's house, you must bring a hostess gift, although it can be a little trinket instead if you prefer. If you bring flowers it is considered polite to take off the paper or plastic wrapping

Many shops sell small pre-packed present ideas labelled 'instead of a flower', meaning you can buy them as a hostess gift.

before handing them over. Unless the party is in a public place, you will remove the shoes you wore outside at the door, and either pad about in socks or else change into party shoes which you have carried in your bag. This is purely practical; it keeps floors clean longer throughout the year, but is very important in the snowy and muddy winter and spring seasons. Shoe removal is crucial rather than optional, but do bring clean shoes with you to change into for a formal party.

When you arrive, you will probably be offered a welcome drink, often a kind of alcoholic punch, or perhaps a cup of *glögg* at Christmas time. After that the drink often switches to beer or wine which you have with the food. Remember, never have a sip before the host or hostess has offered you a toast.

Swedes, after they have given flowers to their hostess and taken their shoes off, will usually greet the other guests in turn. If they are already acquainted or friends, this is just a simple '*hej*' and perhaps a handshake. If not, they will introduce themselves at the time. The onus for introductions is on the arriving guests, not the host or hostess, so it is important not to miss your time to introduce yourself.

At any semi-formal or seated dinner party, the guests are likely to be given places, or at least be asked to sit alternating male and female, and not near their partners. Whichever man is seated to your left (if you are a woman) or woman seated to your right (if you are a man) is your companion for the evening. The male companion is responsible for pouring the drinks for the female, and if there is dancing, the first dance of the evening should be with your 'table companion'.

Even at informal meals, it is rare for Swedes to eat with their fingers. Not only do they prefer to use cutlery, they prefer to use a knife and fork, and do so with the fork in the left hand and the knife in the right. Americans who can't manage this should develop an ability to ignore raised eyebrows. You may need to explain 'we do it differently' at every meal for a long time. Do not be surprised if someone offers you a butter knife with some butter already on it; and if you are taking your own butter, use the communal butter knife which is left in the butter for the purpose.

Saying Your Thanks

At any meal, whether formal or family, Swedes will thank the cook for the meal, usually saying *Tack för maten* (literally, 'Thanks for the food'). At dinner parties with more than eight guests, it is traditionally the job of the male seated to the left of the hostess to thank her, with a small speech, for the meal on behalf of all the guests.

Toasting

During any festive meal there are likely to be glasses of *snaps* (flavoured shots of pure alcohol) and much toasting or *skåling* in Swinglish. The anatomy of a *skål* is very specific: you should lift your glass to about chest level and nod at everyone at the table in turn, going from right to left, before taking a drink (sometimes a sip and sometimes the whole glass, depending on the drink, the occasion and the company). After the drink you should nod at the others again before putting the glass down. In practice, this is often rather rushed through; otherwise it can take a long time.

At a formal party, nobody should propose a toast before the host does, and women should not drink before the man seated to their left (their dinner companion for the evening) has proposed a toast to her. This is important, particularly if you plan to attend any very formal dinners. At most dinners, the host does propose a welcome toast (with the welcome drink, of course) first, but women and men both drink—and *skål*—when they choose.

At a festive meal, you may well be served a *smörgåsbord*, where you will pick your own meal. The standard order is to start with the fish, move on to the meat and then the hot dishes and then finish with the cheese. The rules to remember are, fish before meat and cold before hot. At any meal, you should finish the food on your plate, but no one should take the last bit of food in the serving dish.

After the meal, and the thank-you for it, there is often a break before dessert is served with coffee. This is usually enough to allow stomachs to recover from the food. If at someone's home, everyone will withdraw to the living room and probably eat the dessert there. Coffee is generally served at the same time. It is not unusual for Swedes to sing at any party, either drinking songs (*snapsvisor*) or special songs for the time of year.

Helan Går

One popular drinking song is called 'Helan Går'. The song is very short, and goes:

> *Helan går, sjung hopp falle rallan rallan lej,*
> *Helan går, sjung hopp falle rallan lej.*
> *Och den som inte helan tar,*
> *Han heller inte halvan får.*
> *Helan går, sjung hopp falle rallan lej.*

Phonetic translation:

> 'Helen gore, shung hop falla rallan rallan lay,
> Helen gore, shung hop falla rallan lay.
> Ock dane sum in ta hellan tar, han heller in ta halv ann fore.
> Helen gore, shung hop falla rallan lay'

In translation this means, 'drink the lot; if you don't you'll never get any more.'

When you hear 'Helan Går' it's time to drink the whole *snaps* glass down. Women and foreigners can avoid this task rather more easily than Swedish men, which is just as well as some of the *snaps* can taste very bitter and all are very strong.

When it is time to leave, you should put on your coat and shoes before you thank your host, though you will have said goodbye to the other guests beforehand. The next time you communicate with your hosts, whether in person, by phone or by letter, don't forget to tell them, "Thank you for last time" (*tack för senast*). This is true even if you don't see them again for months. To be very polite, you should write a special 'thank you' or ring specially to thank your hosts within a week, though this is much less important than saying *tack för senast*.

Coffee and Cake Parties

These are very popular parties in Sweden, for birthdays, name-days, in fact any day you feel like inviting people over. They are, perhaps, an equivalent to 'taking tea' in Britain.

Remember, whenever you drink coffee with Swedes that many do not take milk with their coffee, and will pour coffee into your cup to the rim if you don't remind them to leave some space in the cup for your milk or cream.

However, you are unlikely to have any sandwiches, just coffee and cakes. Traditionally, there will be seven cakes on offer. It's no good pleading a small appetite; to be polite, you must take one of each, and at the beginning of the party. Balancing seven small cakes (often the same size as biscuits or cookies) on one plate is easy compared to eating them all if you've eaten a meal before. Enjoy them—they are almost certainly home-baked and delicious. Nowadays, you are also likely to be served a coffeecake or braided cinnamon bread.

Other Celebrations

When you know Swedes better, you may be invited to celebrate bigger occasions with your new friends. Like most other nationalities, Swedes celebrate birthdays, births and marriages, and will gather together for funerals. It is common for children to have a birthday party (*kalas*) every year. Until recently, these were always at home, but a growing trend is to have them at an indoor play area, or another public place such as a bowling area or museum. A similar menu of hot dogs or hamburgers and either ice cream or an ice-cream cake is served at many children's parties. The guests bring presents for the birthday child (which are immediately ripped open upon the child receiving them) and the children play games. If your child is invited to such a party, you are not expected to be there as well—Swedes are comfortable with allowing their children to go to parties without them. If you give a children's party, you are expected to give out party bags for the children, but in Sweden, these are chiefly filled with sweets or candy.

As children become adults, they are less likely to have parties for their birthdays except for 'even' birthdays, when they turn 30, 40, 50 or 60. This custom was originally only for the 50th birthday (and that is still the most important celebration), but many get together with friends and family for eating, drinking, singing and dancing on their 30th and 40th birthdays as well. The American custom of a big party on the 16th birthday and the British and Australian custom of a big party on the 21st birthday are not common in Sweden.

Other celebrations are often more family oriented. Most babies born in Sweden today are still christened, and the parents will invite their families to a meal after the church service, but Swedes do not have large christening parties. Seventy-five percent of Swedes choose to be confirmed in the Church of Sweden in their early teens, and that is another occasion for a family celebration with a cake and gifts.

Celebrating 'Name Days'

Many Swedes do have 'name days' as well. They are not celebrated in the way they are in some countries, but older Swedes may well mark them by having people over for coffee and cake.

WEDDINGS

Weddings, on the other hand, combine a mixture of family and friends for the church service (still the most popular option) and the dinner and dancing afterwards. The celebrations are similar to those in many other European countries, with sparkling wine, flowers and a traditional bridal waltz to start the dancing. One big difference is that in Sweden, the couple will often have lived together for many years, and their children may also be at the wedding, perhaps as flower-girls or pageboys. w, the bride's friends will often have planned a hen night (*möhippa*) for her and the groom's friends a stag night (*svensexa*) for him, at which both will be given lots to drink and have any number of practical jokes played on them. The day of these parties is a surprise for the bride and groom and, unlike some countries, the bride and groom never plan their own parties. (Nor can they escape the ones their friends plan for them!)

The Lysning

On the Sunday before the wedding, the couple may have a *lysning*, which comes from the now defunct tradition of listening to the wedding banns in church and having a meal with presents afterwards. If you are invited to a *lysning*, you take the couple's wedding present to that party and not to the wedding itself, and it is usually a daytime party with a meal and a few drinks.

On the day of the actual wedding, the bride's family traditionally will welcome the guests to the church and during the service, the bride and groom will walk up the aisle to the altar together, instead of the bride and her father meeting the groom at the altar. They will have exchanged two rings at their engagement, and the bride will usually receive a second gold band during the ceremony. After the service, the couple stands outside the church and all of the guests walk past them and congratulate the happy couple. The reception is usually at another hall or restaurant, where the couple arrive last and are toasted with sparkling wine by their guests. They sit under a bridal arch of flowers during

A Swedish bride and groom sit under their bridal wreath at the top of the table.

the meal, which is interrupted often by speeches and songs. After the meal, the bridal couple may open their presents at the reception, and they will almost certainly waltz together before everyone else joins in. They do not usually disappear before the guests, as in a British wedding, but stay and enjoy the party until late.

Many couples go away on a honeymoon, but this is called a 'wedding trip' in Sweden, whereas the Swedish for honeymoon, *smekmånad*, refers to the first month of marriage no matter where you are. When they return, they are likely to send a wedding photo of themselves to their guests as their thank-you cards.

SETTLING IN

CHAPTER 5

'Get your personal number as soon as you can.
You don't exist in Sweden without a personal number.
At least, you start to doubt your existence without it.'
—Author's advice to friend who was
planning to settle down in Sweden

BEFORE YOU MOVE
Residence and Work Permits

The first thing to sort out before you move is your visa, or permission to stay in Sweden. If your company is transferring you, they will probably arrange this for you. Otherwise, you may apply for a visa based on employment, family connection or studies. Information on applying for asylum is a different situation and it is best to contact either the Immigration Office or the Swedish Embassy directly about this.

If you are a European Union (EU) citizen, you have the right to a work permit in Sweden. You may stay in the country for three months while you look for work. To obtain a residence permit, you must present your passport and proof of your employment to the Immigration Office, with an application for residence. If you are planning to start your own business or work on a freelance or consultancy basis, then a certificate of registration for the business or a consultancy or freelance agreement can replace the certificate of employment.

Work Permit for EU citizens

For details on obtaining a work permit, visit the Immigration Office's website at:

http://www.migrationsverket.se

or contact the Swedish Embassy in your own country.

You may be granted a residence permit for the period of employment, or for five years renewable if the employment is permanent. Once you are working in Sweden with a residence permit, your spouse or partner and any children under 21 or elderly parents who are your dependants may also apply for residence permits, even if they are not EU citizens.

European Union citizens who want to live in Sweden without working can also apply to the police for a residence permit, but must have proof that they can support themselves without state assistance. Usually, proof of bank deposits or else a guarantee from another person that they will support you is enough. Students as well as EU pensioners can also apply for residence permits, as long as they can prove they can support themselves.

If you are in a relationship with a Swedish citizen then you may also be eligible for a residence permit without having a job; you do not have to be married but the Immigration Office must be convinced of the stability of the relationship.

Immigration Without EU Membership

If you are not an EU national, it is not as simple. Immigration controls are very strict and unless you have a family or a strong business connection in Sweden, it is unlikely you will be able to move here. The family connection can be with a Swedish resident, rather than a Swedish citizen. Dependent children (under 21), dependent parents and spouses are the most likely to be admitted.

If you are in a relationship with a Swedish citizen (which does not have to be marriage), you can apply for a residence permit as a common law spouse. Application should be made from outside of Sweden, at the Swedish embassy or consulate in your country. Both you and your partner will be asked to fill out forms and will be interviewed separately; your partner in Sweden and you at the embassy/consulate in your country. A residence permit will normally be granted for six months, though it is renewable once in Sweden. You can continue applying for the six-monthly permits, or apply for a permanent permit. If you are not granted a permanent one, you will normally receive another six-month permit. In every case, allow at least six to eight weeks for your application to be processed by the embassy or consulate.

Documents You Will Need

All visitors to Sweden require a valid passport for entry. Depending on your situation you may also need proof of employment, of valid funds to support yourself, or of your relationship with a Swedish citizen. When you have reached Sweden, you may find it useful to have all documentation relating to your education with you, as well as any written employment references. In addition, have your birth certificate, any marriage certificate, driving licence and any other official papers with you. Swedish authorities, educational institutions and employers like to see official copies of documentation. You can have official copies made at the local Employment Office in Sweden (it needs to be signed by an official who can certify it is a copy of the original).

PERSONAL NUMBER (PERSONNUMMER)

If you plan to live in Sweden for any length of time, you must register with the authorities. To do so, take your passport with your work/resident permit information to the tax authorities (Skatteverket), and be ready to fill out some forms. The clerks there will help you if your Swedish is still weak or non-existent. You must register with both the local tax office and with the social insurance authorities (Försäkringskassan).

You will then be issued with a personal number (*personnummer*) which is vital for living in Sweden—you quote it for work, for your bank, at the doctor's, and when using a credit card in many shops. You will need this number before you can register for Swedish language lessons or any social benefits, before you can receive any medical care and before you can open a bank account. Your children will need their numbers before they can start school or childcare or receive medical care.

How to Read Your Personnummer

The number will consist of six digits (your date of birth),
a dash, and then four digits which are your personal number
and differentiates you from others with the same birth date.
For example, someone born on 1 April 1996, might have the
number 960401-2938. The second to last digit is even for females
and odd for males. However, this convention may be changing to
a random selection of numbers for immigrants.

CITIZENSHIP

Once you have lived in Sweden for two years, you are eligible
to vote in local elections. Once you have lived in Sweden for
five years, you can apply for Swedish citizenship. Sweden
now allows dual citizenship but your home country may not
so you should look into this carefully.

There are three ways of becoming a Swedish citizen:
through birth, through naturalisation, and through application.
Any child born to a Swedish mother, or to a Swedish father
who is married to the child's mother, is entitled to Swedish
citizenship. If the child's parents are unmarried, and the
father is Swedish, the child is entitled to Swedish citizenship
if born in Sweden, or, if born overseas, can become entitled
to citizenship if the parents subsequently marry.

To become a citizen through naturalisation, you must have
lived in Sweden for five years (or two years if you are from
one of the other Nordic countries), be over 18 and have
no criminal record. Former Swedish citizens can be
granted citizenship again after two years of residency,
on application.

WHAT TO BRING WITH YOU

There are no restrictions on the amount of foreign currency
you can import into Sweden. It is a good idea to take all of
your important documentation with you, such as your birth
certificates, any educational certificates and an international
driver's licence, and to set up a power of attorney in your
home country if you are leaving a business or a house
behind you.

Aside from the clothing and personal effects you would normally bring with you, you may like to stock up on things which are more difficult or expensive to buy in Sweden. When bringing electrical appliances, be sure of their compatibility with Swedish circuits—Swedish electricity is 220 volts, and plugs usually have two round prongs; you'll find it easier to buy converters and adaptors in your home country before you come. If you have a lot of American electrical goods to bring with you, you may find it cost-effective to buy a frequency converter which allows you to install 110 volts sockets (do make sure it is grounded and your house insurance covers it). This is unlikely to be worthwhile unless your appliances are already expensive; if they are standard then you may as well buy new in Sweden. If you are shipping furniture, remember that Swedish apartments and houses are, in general, smaller than those in North America or Australia/New Zealand.

You may also like to pack an extra supply of English reading material (widely available but not cheap in Sweden) and favourite foods from your own country. If possible, order any magazine or newspaper subscriptions that you'd like before you move. You are allowed to import up to three months' worth of medicine for personal use only. Doing this will buy you time to find out which Swedish equivalent works for you. If you drink alcohol, import the maximum allowed from your part of the world.

What Not to Bring

Don't bother to pack televisions or video recorders—they are not likely to be compatible with the Swedish ones. If you want to bring video cassettes from the United States, however, you will have to bring your video recorder with you because the cassettes are not compatible with the Swedish PAL system. You won't be able to record on a foreign VCR but you may be able to play the tape back. You may not be able to play American DVDs on a Swedish DVD player either, because of territorial restrictions, unless you have a region-free DVD player. Telephones can be imported, but not mobile phones. Remember, also, that you do not need to take your refrigerator, freezer or oven with you; Swedes leave these behind when they move away, so there will already be one in your new home.

Don't take fresh meats, dairy produce or eggs without permission, or illegal drugs and restricted animal products, such as ivory. If in doubt, check with the embassy first.

You can import your car to Sweden even if it is a left-hand drive. To register it, you are required to ensure it is up to Swedish environmental standards, have it inspected and insure it. If you sell the car within a year, you will have to pay import duties on it. You may find it easier to buy a Swedish car after you move, unless you have a particularly special car (i.e. expensive, antique, etc). Having said this, most Europeans will import their own vehicles, and if you are shipping a full container transcontinentally, you may like to investigate shipping your car within it.

> ### Information on Importing Goods
> For specific importing information contact The Swedish Transport Agency at http://www.transportstyrelsen.se. Most information is in Swedish only, but you can contact them for the information you need in English.

PETS

If you are moving to Sweden temporarily, consider finding a short-term home for your pet rather than taking it with you. Animal immigration regulations are strict and your pet may have to be quarantined at one of the quarantine stations in Stenungsund, Sollefteå, Furuland and Vallentuna. You may need to obtain an import permit, issued by the National Board for Agriculture (Jordbruksverket). This involves your vet granting your dog or cat a pet passport (in your home country), identifying your pet with a tattoo or an implanted microchip, and treating your pet against internal parasites shortly before you move. In some instances, your pet may need a rabies vaccination (depending on your country). If you are importing your pet from a so-called 'high risk' country (ie, a country where the risk of rabies is deemed to be high), the animal may need to be quarantined.

National Board for Agriculture

For up-to-date information on details and procedures for bringing your pet into Sweden, including their current list of 'high risk' countries, contact the National Board for Agriculture at their website:

http://www.sjv.se.

Or write to them at:

Jordbruksverket, 55182

Jönköping, Sweden

FINDING A PLACE TO LIVE

The standard of housing in Sweden is high, with most homes having central heating, good insulation and modern plumbing. Around half of Swedes live in a house, with the rest living in apartments. Most apartments are housed in blocks of flats, rather than in converted houses. Houses are commonly either terraced (row) houses or else detached houses. The traditional wooden houses are back in fashion after many years of modern designs, though in all homes, natural sunlight and clean interiors add the feel of simplicity that is typical of Swedish design.

Most Swedish homes will include a fridge, a freezer and a washing machine. Practical work areas and storage spaces are a priority. Most flats will have a specific storage area either attached to the flat or else in the basement of the block, and a special laundry room. With good insulation and double-, triple- or sometimes quadruple-glazed windows, there is no need to draw the curtains at night to keep away the cold, and few Swedes do.

Most homes are furnished comfortably but in style. Swedes appreciate good design and enjoy their rural roots, which is evident in their style of interior design. You will often see traditional elements such as wooden *köksoffor* (kitchen benches) or folk-painted brooms within a very modern design. Swedish homes are often filled with houseplants.

Many Swedish households are made up of just one or two people, with many young adults leaving home early and fewer elderly people moving in with their extended families. Many communities of flats and rowhouses are built around a playground area and common buildings for laundry facilities and bicycle storage. In spite of this, in urban areas it's not unusual for neighbours not to know each other, although many say they would welcome friendly neighbours.

These blocks of apartments offer a green common area between them. Places for children to play and for everyone to relax are considered important for flat dwellers.

There are three main ways of finding a home in Sweden: renting a flat; partly buying a flat or a house—paying an initial deposit (*insats*) and then a monthly rent (*hyran*); or buying a house outright. About 40 per cent of all homes are rented, and tenants are protected under Swedish law against unfair rent increases. The law also ensures that you may not be charged significantly more for your flat than for a similar one in the same building. The rent generally includes heating and maintenance, including redecorating at reasonable intervals of time.

To rent a flat, you can either go through a private agency, or *bostadsföretag*; through a public housing company; or sublet from the owner or first tenant (a sublet flat is called an *andrahand*—second-hand flat). You can find the private agencies in the telephone book, but they may charge a fee for their services. Nearly half of all rented accommodation in Sweden is owned by the public housing companies. You may have to put your name on a waiting list to get a flat in a certain area, and particularly in Stockholm and Göteborg, you may have to start out by renting a sublet. There are often long waiting lists. The sublet flats are advertised in the local papers, or else people hear about them via contacts. You will have to sign a contract for a fixed amount of time for a sublet, and some flats have restrictions on how long they can be sublet for. It is less common to rent a house but certainly possible—check the newspapers or with an estate agent (*fastigshetsmäklare*).

Buying a Place

To buy a flat or house, go through the realty agents. You can find them listed in the yellow pages of the telephone directory, which is called Gula Sidorna in Sweden. The yellow pages are also online at:

http://www.gulasidorna.se

You can find most of the real estate agents online as well.

If you buy a flat or a house which includes use of common areas (i.e. laundry areas, common gardens, etc.), you will

The kind of kitchen many Swedes aspire to. Clean lines, modern appliances and a table in the kitchen are all common elements of Swedish kitchens, but most are smaller than this one.

have to pay a deposit to actually buy the property, but still pay a monthly rent to cover maintenance and upkeep on the building (for a flat) and/or the common areas. Often, you will also sign an agreement that restricts what you can do with your property, usually concerning renting it out, using it for business, or renovating it. If you buy a house outright, you do not have to pay rent but you are, of course, solely responsible for the building and grounds.

Mortgages are similarly arranged as in most other Western countries. However, the terms of repayment are often a good deal longer; 50-year mortgages are not unusual. In addition, you can choose to have variable or fixed rate, or to combine them, borrowing a proportion of the money on a fixed rate and the remainder on a variable. It can be easier to arrange a mortgage than a mobile phone contract, as long as you have a deposit and proof of employment.

> **Home-owner's Responsibilities**
>
> Note that Swedes are safety conscious in the home and many install smoke alarms and security alarms to guard against accidents and break-ins. It is your responsibility to ensure the pavements and walkways in front of your house are safe for passers-by; this includes clearing them of snow, leaves or grit as needed.

HOUSEHOLD FURNISHINGS

If you have not imported your entire household, you may need to buy some inexpensive furnishings quickly. You could do worse than follow the Swedish lead and head for IKEA, the chain of household furnishings which was founded in Småland in 1942 by Ingvar Kamprad. It has long been the most affordable place in Sweden to buy furniture, kitchen goods, fabric (for curtains and upholstery), kitchen and bathroom fittings, lighting and decorations. A warning here—no matter which branch you visit, it will be crowded every weekend. However, you can take a lot of the furniture home with you (because it is often flatpack, self assembly furniture). If you can't, then they will deliver for free within a certain radius of the shop.

Other national shops which sell household goods include Åhléns (a general department store selling food, clothing, gifts and household goods) and, in Göteborg and Stockholm,

NK (short for Nordiska Kompaniet) which is rather more expensive. For china, glass, crockery and other tableware, Duka is one of the best national shops, while less expensive alternatives include Coop Forum.

Another option is to frequent the auction houses and second-hand shops. Most towns have at least one second-hand shop which sells goods to raise money for *u-hjälpen* (assistance for the developing world) or for a church or athletic club. The furniture, crockery, clothing and so on ranges widely in quality, age and price, from expensive antiques (at the auction house) to rickety old stools which need painting. You can often find many things you need much cheaper in the second-hand shops. Look also online at http://www.tradera.se, which is the Swedish ebay or http://www.blocket.se where people advertise second hand goods.

BANKS AND MONEY
Currency

The Swedish currency is the crown, called krona (plural kronor) in Swedish, and öre. Two abbreviations often used are 'SEK', placed in front of the number, or 'Kr' placed afterwards. The money system is metric, with 100 öre making up a crown, although öre are no longer used and the smallest coin is for 1 crown. Other coins include the 5 crown and 10 crown coins. Notes are in denominations of 20, 50, 100, 500, 1000 and 10,000 crowns. Some larger shops in tourist areas may accept euros, British sterling and/or American dollars as payment as well.

Sweden is one of the countries which has rejected the euro, along with Denmark and Britain. The latest referendum on the subject was held in September 2003, although it is likely that another referendum will be held at some point in the future.

If you are exchanging money in Sweden, one of the better rates of exchange is at the Forex (foreign exchange) counters in the larger cities. If you keep your receipt, you will be able to exchange your Swedish currency back into your home currency without paying a commission at any Forex counter. You may not export more than 6,000 kronors in Swedish currency. It is relatively simple to transfer money from an overseas bank to a Swedish one, and can take as little as a day from either Britain or the US, but you may be charged both a transfer and a currency exchange fee depending on your bank's policy. If you can, carry as much money as you will want with you when you move, preferably in traveller's cheques, for depositing into your bank account. There are other ways of transferring money, via agents. This information changes regularly and it is worthwhile asking for up-to-date advice from your bank.

Opening a bank account is easy, but you may need a personal number to do it. There are different types of accounts and the staff at the bank should be able to advise you on which is best for you. Transfer of money between accounts at Swedish banks is simple and fast, and most bills are paid by bank transfer. You do this by filling out bank transfer forms with the accounts payable and sending the forms to your bank. When the funds have been transferred, your bank sends notification to the payee. This system replaces cheques for most Swedes, and cheques are not widely used. Note that it is difficult to deposit a foreign cheque into a Swedish bank; the length of time it takes to clear and the fee charged make it frustrating.

Most bank accounts will issue you with a cash machine card, so that you can obtain money from a cash machine in the wall of the bank after hours, and you may also find an account card (*kontokort*) useful. This card works like a credit card when paying for goods and services but the money is transferred directly out of your account.

> In Sweden, it is normal for your salary to be paid directly into your bank account. Your pay packet will consist of a pay advice slip, letting you know how much has been deposited into your account.

As in many countries, Internet banking has become very popular and many Swedes run their accounts online.

Taxation

The Swedish taxation system works on a pay as you earn basis, so your pay slip will already have income tax deducted from it. Your bank will also deduct taxes from the interest you earn as necessary. Swedish taxes are based on the municipality in which you live, although there is also a national tax, at a higher rate, for high earners. The average, otherwise, is between 30–33 per cent. Indirect taxation is high compared with many other countries, with a value-added tax (MOMS) of 25 per cent on most goods and services. Food, medicines and books have a lower MOMS rating, while alcohol has a higher one. Depending on what country you come from, and how long you intend to stay in Sweden, you should check that you will have home tax relief because of paying tax in Sweden. Many countries have double tax agreements (among them the UK and the US) and many European countries will also have social security agreements, so that you can apply social security payments made in Sweden to your home country's system.

Brief Guide to Benefits

Although the taxes are high, remember that you are entitled to a range of benefits in exchange for them. Several which result in financial payouts are child benefit, parental leave and housing benefit.

- If you earn under a certain amount you can apply for housing benefit to help pay your rent.
- You can also claim child benefit for each child under 16 years of age (this is not means-tested and all are eligible), and can take paid time off work after the birth of a child.
- You may also be entitled to parental leave pay even if you have not worked in Sweden before, although the amount will be small.

For any of these you must be registered with the tax authorities for a certain time before you are eligible. Check with the Insurance Office (Försäkringskassan) for details of these and other benefits.

HEALTH CARE

Another major benefit in Sweden is heavily subsidised health care (free for children or students under age 19). If you need emergency health care in Sweden, visit a hospital emergency department (not all hospitals will accept emergencies so it is worth telephoning ahead to check). As long as you are registered in the Swedish social system, you need only give your personal number to be treated. For regular medical care, however, you should make an appointment to see the duty doctor at the local health centre (Vårdcentral) when you feel ill. You can sometimes get an immediate appointment if it is urgent; but for a real emergency, you should always go to the hospital. Care between different health centres varies widely; some offer drop-in clinics for all while others require appointments and treat only those in their geographical area. Although health care is heavily subsidised in Sweden, you will need to pay a fee for a doctor's appointment. You can receive a 'high cost card'; if you pay up to the ceiling on that for doctors' fees then you pay no more in that 12-month period.

The exception to paying a fee is if you need to see a midwife in the Mother's Health Care Centre (Mödrarvårdscentralen). At this centre you can receive advice and prescriptions for contraception as well as pre- and post-natal care. You will need to go to the centre in your area—check the municipal pages of the phone directory for information. Contraception is readily available in Sweden. Abortion is a right in Sweden and is free on request up until the end of the 18th week of pregnancy. There is no stigma attached to using contraception, abortion or choosing to have a child out of wedlock.

Pharmacies

Should you get a prescription from your doctor or midwife, you will need to visit the chemist or pharmacy, which is called Apoteket in Sweden. This has been a monopoly for years and still is at time of writing. However, the monopoly is likely to disappear halfway through 2009. They also sell shampoos, soaps, toothpastes and other similar items, but these are also sold in supermarkets and are often cheaper there. To buy something at an Apoteket, you must take a number when you go in, then wait for it to be called. There may be different number queues for prescription and non-prescription assistance; look for *recept* (prescription) or *receptfritt* (non-prescription). Prescriptions are often filled while you wait, and are subsidised by the state so are not too expensive. If you need to buy a lot of a medicine (for example, for an ongoing condition), you can obtain a card to show how much you have spent on medicine. Once you have spent over a certain amount within a calendar year, all other medicine you need for your personal use will be free that year.

If you don't have a prescription, you follow the same procedure and ask the chemist for advice. They have excellent training and you can often avoid paying to see a doctor if you have a common complaint, as they can provide you with the cure. However, many drugs which do not require a prescription elsewhere are regulated in Sweden. For example, strong cough medicines which you can buy over the counter in the United States, Australia and the United Kingdom are only available on prescription in Sweden. Antibiotics which are widely available in Asia are also regulated.

Dental Care

Seeing a dentist in Sweden is similar to most other countries: you ring up a dentist and ask for an appointment. Dental treatment is also subsidised but dentists are free to set their own prices and these can vary enormously. The Insurance Office has guidelines on the price differences and advises patients to check the prices in advance. There is a higher subsidy on dental care for adults between 20–29 and over the age of 60—these patients pay slightly cheaper rates. There is also a public dentist who provides free dental care for children, and can offer adult care as well; these are often among the less expensive dentists to visit. You can find dentists in the telephone book under 'Tandvård'.

Children up to the age of 19 receive free health care, dental treatment and eye checkups, as well as subsidised eyeglasses if needed.

EDUCATION

Formal schooling for Swedish children begins when they are seven and if you have children between the ages of 7–16, they are required by law to attend school. However, every child aged four or five has the right to 15 hours of preschool per week. Many of these children are already enrolled in a preschool (day care centres are preschools in Sweden and the staff are trained preschool teachers) because their parents work. For any who are not, there is a local preschool available for them (*allmän förskola*). Early childhood education is generally considered an advantage for both educational and socialising opportunities for children. You can also choose childcare from a childminder or in a 'family home' environment but it is less common.

Childcare costs in Sweden are heavily subsidised through a *maxtaxa* reform which stipulates a low ceiling on how much any family has to pay for childcare. This was both to help parents have more freedom to work and also create more educational opportunities for children. In most municipalities, children can keep their childcare places when their parents are on parental leave caring for a younger sibling, or if they are unemployed. Many argue that this reform has lead to larger groups of children and worse care. In addition, some municipalities have long queues for day care. Nevertheless, the standards of childcare are still very high and at any preschool, you can expect the children to have a great deal of outdoor playtime, quiet reading time, social meal time, and opportunities for singing, arts and crafts, cooking and playing with toys. Most preschools offer regular outings to the woods or to such events as children's theatre performances.

From the autumn of the year in which a child turns six, he or she will generally attend a final preschool year at the primary school. It feels like the start of 'real' school but is still not compulsory and is meant to be a relaxed year of learning about school, and is referred to as the F (for *förskoleklass*) year, or informally as Year 0. Class groups are made up of all children born in the same year, so the cut-off date is the 31 December, rather than a date in August or September.

Parents can choose to start their children a year earlier, in consultation with the school, or a year later should their child not be ready to start yet.

In general, a child starts compulsory school in the year in which he or she turns seven. Until recently, compulsory schooling was broken up into three divisions of three years each: primary school (*lågstadiet*), middle school (*mellanstadiet*) and high school (*högstadiet*). There are still nine years of compulsory schooling but the traditional divisions have now gone. However, there are national tests for students in Years 3, 5 and 9. The curriculum is currently being reviewed, a process due for completion by 2011. One proposal being considered is the addition of an optional 10th year of schooling for students who may need more preparation before senior secondary school. This educational reform began in the 1995–1996 school year and, again, is under review.

The majority of children attend state comprehensive schools for their compulsory schooling. However, the number of independent schools (*friskolor*) is growing and there is a very small but growing band of home schoolers. The school authority inspects the independent schools as well and they receive grants so that few charge any fees at all. There are several international schools—teaching in English or other foreign languages—in the larger cities, as well as some religious schools. For children who are particularly talented in sport or music, there are specialised schools with restricted admission where they will study the ordinary school subjects but have their studies scheduled around extra time for practices, games and recitals. Single sex schools are not common in Sweden.

The school year is broken up into two semesters, with Christmas and summer holidays in between them. The autumn semester starts earlier than in most European countries, in late August, breaks usually in late

Compulsory Subjects

Certain subjects are compulsory in Swedish schools, among them mathematics, Swedish, English, social studies (including geography, history and religion), science (including biology, chemistry and physics) and physical education. Both boys and girls learn home economics and handicraft so that boys can sew and girls can carve wood. In addition, there are many elective subjects, such as other foreign languages.

October/early November and ends at Christmas time. The spring semester breaks twice—once for a 'sports holiday' in February, and once at Easter. The actual dates of the holidays are staggered throughout different school areas, so that not all school children are on holiday at once, except in the summer, Easter and Christmas holidays. Schools are in session from early morning to either midday or mid-afternoon, Monday to Friday.

Many children take part in after-school activities. Up to the age of ten or 12, it is usual to attend after-school care at the school, who will have trained staff to look after the children. After that, there are after-school clubs or else families make their own arrangements. In addition, it is usual for children to take part in sporting, music, religious or cultural groups or instruction after school, often with very full schedules. Such activities as sports teams are not centred around the schools in Sweden, but rather around separate sports clubs.

After finishing compulsory schooling, usually at the age of 15 or 16, over 95 per cent of all students continue to further their education through a gymnasium. At this point in time, students specialise and can choose vocational, technical or academic lines, depending on where their interests lie. For some academic lines, students will need high marks from their final years in school. It is possible to study an international curriculum, leading to A-Levels, SATs or the International Baccalaureate.

Books, lunches and transport to and from the local schools are provided free of charge for all schools and gymnasiums. The dress code and discipline is relaxed, making for a generally friendly and pleasant atmosphere. Competition is not emphasised in Swedish schools as much as co-operation in learning, and this aspect of Swedish education has its critics who say that the system discourages high achievers. The natural counter-argument is that co-operation fosters learning. This argument leads to several often debated subjects, such as that of grades and standardised tests, and whether children should be graded at all.

Another debate is whether the role of a teacher is to hand down knowledge or lead students to discovering

Founded in 1666, Lund University is Sweden's largest institute of higher learning and research.

knowledge themselves. The Swedish educational system is now working to balance the newer ideas of co-operative teaching with the call for back-to-basics teaching, so that students will benefit by receiving the best of both systems.

Students who want to study further after *gymnasium* can choose one of over 30 universities and places of higher education, and over 40 per cent do go on to further study. Subjects studied range again from vocational through to academic. Tuition is free, but students pay for their own board, lodging and books, often through a government-sponsored student loan system. Most courses last between three and five years, depending on subject and qualification. They can choose to study a programme leading to a specific exam, or else a modular degree.

Adult Education

There is ample provision in Sweden for adults who want to continue to study, even if they did not choose to continue to higher education directly from school. The Adult Education system (Komvux for short) offers courses both in subjects which can build towards university entrance and in vocational subjects for training towards a different career. These courses carry no course fee, and students can apply for study grants to compensate for lost income. Note that in some instances you cannot apply for these grants before you have been resident for two years in Sweden (exceptions are made for permanent residence permits). In addition to the municipal- and state-run adult education courses, there are many private educational centres offering different courses, which do charge fees.

Immigrants are entitled to free Swedish language instruction, and children of immigrants can receive both extra Swedish language instruction for school work as well as extra lessons in their native language. This is to encourage them to become bilingual. (*For more details on this, see* Chapter Eight: Swinglish or Svengelska?, *page 198.*)

COMMUNICATION

Sweden has adopted both mobile phone and Internet communications more quickly and effectively than many nations. A very high percentage of Swedes own mobile phones and will often use these as much or more than a land line. However, most Swedish homes still have a land line. When you sign up for a telephone you will need to pay a connection charge and then a quarterly account. You can request an itemised account if you want.

Sweden's telephone directories are comprehensive, and include residential, business, municipal services and regional services sections. There are usually detailed local maps at the beginning of the directory, and the yellow pages (Gula Sidorna) list businesses by category.

The largest telephone company, although state owned, works as a private corporation and the market is now open for

Important Information

- If you are calling from a phone box, you can use a disposable phone card (available at newsagents and kiosks), or you may find a box which still takes coins (less commonly). Some phones will also take credit cards.
- There are no collect calls within Sweden, although you can make collect calls overseas through your home operator by dialling 02-079 first.
- The code for overseas calls is '00'.
- For directory assistance call 118-118.
- Numbers starting with '020' are freephone calls.
- The international country code is 46.
- The emergency services telephone number is 112, and you will need to be able to tell the operator what has happened, which emergency service you need, and where you are calling from. Don't panic if you can't speak Swedish; operators will do their best in English.

other companies. Competition for both residential and business customers in recent years has driven down telephone bills markedly, and when choosing a telephone service you should shop around. Some offer different packages with varying amounts of free or reduced price calls.

More and more people are exploring free telephony via Internet websites. One of the largest services, skype, was co-founded by the Swede Niklas Zennström. As in many other countries, SMS or text messaging via mobile phones is very common as well.

Emailing is prevalent, both because of the interconnectedness of Swedes and the high cost of the postal service. Most official business you may need to conduct can be done by downloading forms via the Internet or by logging into a remote system. Many authorities discourage phone calls by limiting telephone times.

The Swedish postal system is efficient, if expensive. There are no longer any post offices; but bookshops, general stores and supermarkets will often sell stamps and weigh the parcels you want to send. There is one postal delivery a day on weekdays, with none on weekends. All Swedish addresses include a five digit postal code, which will speed up your post. If you live in a block of flats, your address may be the same as the other five flats in your block. People writing to you should put your full name on the letter, and you should put your name on the door of your flat or house (or on your postbox) so that the postal worker can find you. If you receive a parcel, you will generally receive a slip of paper notifying you that you can collect it at the nearest collection point (the nearest general store, bookshop or supermarket, generally).

GETTING AROUND

Because Sweden is so sparsely populated many Swedes drive private cars to get around. However, public transport between cities and towns and within urban areas is very good, with a bus system operating in most areas. Local public transport includes buses, trams, trains and ferries, particularly in the Stockholm and Göteborg areas. In many cities and towns, you

Even in the mountains, the Swedes stay connected.

The bus system in Sweden is efficient and safe.

can buy a season ticket for a day, a week, a month or a year for a particular area or route. In addition, taxis in cities are plentiful, as strict drink driving rules mean that few Swedes drive for an evening out on the town, and the fares are not expensive if shared among several people.

Long Distance Travel

For long distances, the Swedish national railways (SJ, which stands for Statens Järnvägar) run regional, intercity and express trains. Larger stations will have touch-sensitive maps where you can get travel information and ticket prices in English; otherwise you can approach the ticket sellers who will usually know some English. The trains are comfortable and punctual, though they can be expensive. On night trains, you can book a sleeper (with a couchette).

The coach system means that smaller towns and villages not on the railroads are accessible, and the tickets are generally cheaper than train tickets. The coaches stop more often, and some are request stops only, which means you

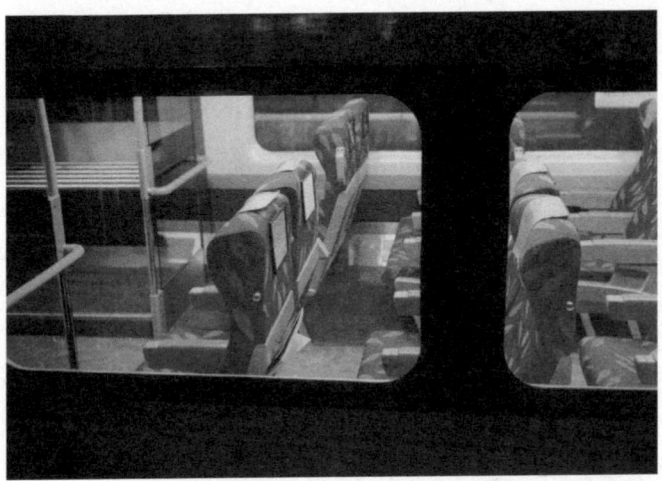

The Arlanda Express runs from the centre of Stockholm to the city's main airport in Arlanda.

need to look out for your stop and ask the driver for it before you get there. The domestic air service is less frequently used (except by businesspeople) for the shorter distances, but is comprehensive. Scandinavian Airline System (SAS) is the national airline (it's also the national airline for the other Scandinavian countries) and flies hourly between Stockholm and Göteborg, with regular flights throughout the rest of Sweden. There are sometimes very cheap deals for passengers under 26, or stand-by on the last flight of the night. In addition, more and more budget airlines are starting up.

If you choose to drive long distances, you may notice on road maps that there are a lot of lakes and bays without bridges which you have to cross. These are served by regular car ferries, some of which are free (those considered part of the road) and other which charge a fee (usually those where you have a choice of going around but take the ferry to save time). Larger ferries between the mainland and Scandinavian islands do cost money, and often need to be booked in advanced, particularly in the summer months.

Driving in Sweden
If you plan to drive in Sweden, you need to carry your full licence with you whilst driving. European Union licences are

accepted for the length of their validity, however long you live in Sweden, but any other licence needs to be replaced by a Swedish one within a year of registering yourself as a resident in Sweden. You can exchange a European Union, Swiss or Japanese licence directly for a Swedish one. However, drivers from other countries will need to pass a written test (which you can take in English), a driving test (with a manual transmission) and a winter driving test (in which you drive on ice and your winter driving skills—especially your turning and stopping skills—are assessed) in order to obtain a Swedish licence. You must be at least 18 years old to drive a car in Sweden. For up to date information on getting a Swedish driving licence, see http://www.korkortsportalen.se and click on 'Andra språk' for English language information.

Swedes drive on the right, and keep car headlamps on at all times. Seat belts are required in the front and back, and children under seven should be in harnesses or child-seats. Remember that safety is paramount in Sweden. Drink driving rules are very strict, and you can be stopped at random and

Swedes drive on the right and keep their headlights on at all times. Speed limits are relatively low and roads are not that congested outside of the cities.

asked to take a breathalyser test. The blood alcohol limit is 0.02 per cent, and you are likely to receive a fine, lose your licence and face possible imprisonment if you are over the limit, so don't drink and drive.

The roads are generally uncrowded, except in the cities. The speed limits are low for Europe: 110 kmph (68 mph) on motorways; 90 kmph (56 mph) on larger roads; and 70 or 50 kmph (43 or 31 mph) in built up areas and in towns. Watch out for both pedestrians and cyclists (there are more on Swedish roads than you may be used to) and also for wild animals in rural areas. One encounter with a moose is likely to be one more than your car can handle, and both reindeer and elk wander across roads from time to time. There are usually signs to warn you.

In the winter, you will need winter tyres which have deeper treads and sometimes studs, especially in the north. You are not allowed to keep these on your car in the summertime, and a date is set every spring after which you cannot drive with them on your car (usually 1 April or 1 May, depending on the region and the severity of the winter). They are allowed again after another date in the autumn, also set annually.

Many petrol stations operate automatic pumps, where you deposit notes or a credit card into the pump to make it work. There are, of course, staffed self service stations as well.

Buying a Car

If you choose to buy a car in Sweden you need to register it in your name, pay a road tax and have the car inspected annually. You are required by law to have third party insurance for it. For more information about the details of this and for obtaining a driving licence, contact the Swedish Road Administration (Vägverket) at tel: (0771) 119-119 or log onto their website at:
http://www.vv.se/

Bicycles

For an often cold and snowy country, Swedes cycle a lot, and it's probably for a combination of reasons. It allows Swedes

Swedish cities have special clearly marked bicycle paths that only bicycles can travel on. These are separate from normal traffic and are thus safer for the cyclists.

Don't be surprised to discover that your colleague cycles to work. The bicycle is a cheaper alternative transport, plus it is good for the environment and promotes health. Small wonder the Swedes appreciate it so much.

to be outdoors, stay healthy and keep the environment clean. More crucially, it is cheaper. Cycling in Swedish cities is made much easier by excellent cycle paths, often separated from car traffic, and with special traffic lights for cycle traffic. There are many long distance cycle paths linking towns and cities the length of Sweden.

You can buy second-hand bicycles through adverts in the papers or at bicycle shops. Buy a good lock at the same time and lamps, which are required after dusk. Reflectors are also required, but most bikes will come equipped with them. Helmets, baskets, panniers and a bell to warn pedestrians of your approach are other useful purchases. Children up to the age of 15 are required to wear helmets whilst cycling.

Many of the bicycle paths can also be used by mopeds, which are popular among the youngsters. You can drive a moped from the age of 15 in Sweden, and a helmet is required for it. Motorcycles must use the ordinary roads,

The Njupeskär waterfall at Fulufjället National Park is the largest waterfall in Sweden. It stands at a height of over 90 metres.

Stortorget (The Big Square) is an old public square located in Stockholm. Its cobbled streets are lined with many historical and significant buildings, making it a popular destination for tourists.

Forestry is an important industry in Sweden. Apart from providing employment for many people, 11 per cent of Sweden's total industrial value also comes from the paper industry, which relies on forest products.

The Ales Stenar (Ale's Stones) is an ancient monument found in the southern province of Skåne. Formed by 59 large boulders in the shape of a ship, mystery continues to surround the monument regarding its exact purpose.

The *knäckebröd* (Swedish crispbread) is typically made from ingredients such as rye flour, salt and yeast. This unique bread type is considered a staple food in Sweden.

meant for cars. Motorcyclists need a special licence (for which they must be over 18) and are required to wear helmets as well. However, you can drive a 125cc light motorcycle from the age of 16 but a special licence is required.

CONSUMER INFORMATION

Shopping in Sweden can be expensive, due to the value added tax (*moms*). It is 25 per cent on most goods in Sweden, although some are taxed at a reduced rate of 12 per cent or 6 per cent, e.g. books. Food is taxed at only 12 per cent and alcohol taxed at variable rates higher than 25 per cent. You may prefer to buy things when you make visits home or to neighbouring countries. Many Swedes stock up on day or weekend trips to Denmark, Germany, Poland, or the Baltic countries. (Norway and Finland are even more expensive.) If you are only in Sweden for a short time (and if you are exporting the goods out of the European Union), you can receive the *moms* back when you leave the country. Most shops will have the 'Tax-free for Tourists' sign in the window; just ask the sales assistant for help with it.

Shopping Hours and Information

Most shops are still open only during the working week, which means 10:00 am to 6:00 pm from Monday to Friday and 9:00 am to 5:00 pm on Saturdays, though this is often much longer in the bigger cities. In larger shopping centres, they may have extended shopping hours and Sunday shopping as well.

Paying by cash is common, but not as common any more as paying with a plastic card—either a credit card or a debit card drawn directly out of a bank account. Cheques are not at all common in Sweden and it is unlikely that many shops will accept one as payment.

If you want to return goods which you have bought at a shop, you have a few options. If you know you may want to return them when you buy them, make sure you tell the shop assistant. He or she may then write the words *öppet köp* on your receipt, and will tell you how many days you have to decide. This means literally 'open purchase' which will

This outdoor flower shop in Stockholm's Gamla Stan is one of the places which you might want to shop at.

enable you to get a refund without any questions. If you do not ask for *öppet köp* then it is up to the goodwill of the shop owner; you do not have any rights of return unless the goods are damaged. This is different from many shops worldwide, which offer no hassle refunds as a matter of course. Shops in Sweden which advertise a no-hassle refund policy usually only honour this policy if you have asked for *öppet köp* in the first place.

However, if you are returning goods which are faulty or damaged, then you are protected under Swedish law, and must be offered either a refund or another item. Many electrical or mechanical goods are also sold with manufacturers' guarantees, so that if something subsequently breaks, you can receive a replacement.

In general, shop assistants in Sweden are helpful and many will either speak English or try to help you through sign language. You are often encouraged to try clothing on, to listen to CDs and tapes, or to try out sports equipment within the shop, before you buy, but it goes against Swedish nature to pressure you into buying anything.

CLOTHING

Depending on where you are moving from, you may need to invest in some good outerwear when you move to Sweden. A jacket, coat or raincoat is essential for much of the year. For winter, you will want a pair of sturdy waterproof boots, lined with wool or fur (though not as often these days) and with good soles for tramping on ice and through snow. Heavy waxed jackets (like Barbour or Drizabone) are also popular because, although it is cold in the winter, it does rain more than snow in the southern and western coastal cities (such as Malmö and Göteborg).

In most offices, workers wear fairly casual clothes; jeans are not uncommon. However, fashion is very important in Sweden, especially in the cities and amongst young people. The rise of inexpensive fashion shops such as Hennes & Mauritz helps fuel this. While everyday work and study clothes are more casual, Swedes are more likely to dress up to go out in the evening or to a party, although

Shopping in Sweden offers you a wide range to choose from. Women's apparel stores offer a variety of clothing, from casual to formal and from inexpensive to designer brand names.

you are unlikely to have much use for a ball gown or dinner jacket.

Sports clothing, both for sports and leisure, is very popular and in general, American clothing is widely available and worn. Swedish sizes are the same as European sizes, and the clothing sold tends to be of a high quality. By Swedish law, every piece of clothing sold must have a tag which gives the composition of the clothing along with instructions on how to wash it. Cotton and wool tend to be preferred to other fabrics, although leather is also popular for outerwear.

CRIME AND THE POLICE

The crime rate in Sweden generally is very low, with the most common offence being drink driving (an effect of the very strict laws). Violent crime is on the increase in Sweden, as in many countries, but gun control is stringent, and most people do not feel their personal security is threatened.

> **Reporting a Crime**
> If you do need to report a crime, ring 112, the general emergency number, and ask for *polislarm* (police alarm).

If you are arrested, you should inform your embassy or consulate immediately. You can be detained for up to 12 hours, and then for a further day after orders from a prosecutor. Everyone is entitled to legal representation in Sweden; the court will appoint a representative for you, or you can request a specific one. There is an extensive legal aid system, and you can request an hour of discounted legal advice from any lawyer.

Sentencing for criminal offences is generally geared toward rehabilitation rather than simple punishment and there is no death penalty in Sweden. The harshest sentence a criminal can receive is lifetime imprisonment but in practice, this generally means between 7–16 years. For lesser crimes, sentences can include fines, community service, between 14 days to 16 years imprisonment, or a combination of these.

Prisoners are offered training, particularly vocational and social, and help in fighting alcohol or drug dependency, to ensure that they can rejoin society when they are released. Some prisoners are also granted leaves without supervision to help them prepare themselves for freedom, while others, particularly young offenders, are taken on character building trips in the countryside. Swedes debate whether these measures should be allowed, or whether correctional care should be stricter.

COMBATING CULTURE SHOCK IN SWEDEN

When moving to any new culture, people often find that the first few months are easier than the next four to six. You'll be busy settling in, finding places to frequent, meeting new friends, and Sweden will seem exotic to you. Take advantage of these first few months to get to know the Swedish way of life a bit better.

The second stage of culture shock takes place when you realise that you are actually living in Sweden and may be there for some time. Anything that you dislike is magnified now, and you're likely to start comparing everything with the way things are back home. (When you start thinking that people pushing on the morning bus commute are actually more polite back home, then you know you're suffering from the second stage!) You seem to have reached a plateau in language learning, so that you can almost get by but don't feel you'll ever really be conversant in Swedish.

Some people think it's a good idea to plan a holiday home within three months. Others think you might suffer even more by comparing your home, where your friends are (and you're on holiday), with Sweden, where you are going through culture shock and working. A good compromise is to invite family or friends to come visit you. You'll relive your first exciting months in Sweden by showing your friends around, making you feel more positive about the place.

The third big stage of culture shock is acculturatisation, which comes gradually. Even while you are still criticising the weather or the food, you will come to accept the Swedish way of life. Your language will improve without your noticing it, and you will make real Swedish friends. If you do eventually go back home, you'll find yourself affected by Swedish values and 'the Swedish way' of doing things.

It is possible to understand and live the Swedish way without abandoning your own culture, and you can do this by socialising with other immigrants, and travelling home regularly. At the same time, you may start to disapprove of certain things in your home country (after all, you've picked up the Swedish value system). But don't disapprove when you're with your old friends and family—they haven't lived through the same culture shock and may not appreciate hearing your new ideas. Be sensitive to this, so that you don't lose your connections with your home country.

How Long Will It Take?

If you have recently moved to Sweden, you may be wondering just how long this adjustment will take. As you've probably guessed, there are no rules about this. From purely personal experience, I have found that people in full-time work similar to their work at home adjust quickest, while children in Swedish schools also help families to adjust. It took most immigrants I knew between six and eight months to feel at home in Sweden, and perhaps another four to six months to settle into the Swedish way of life. People who were transferred to Sweden for work, and knew they would only be in Sweden for a year or two, often maintained the best attitude towards the differences. If you find it very difficult to adjust, try pretending that you will only be in Sweden a short time, so you will take the chance to learn as much as you can about Sweden. It may sound too optimistic, but it works!

How else can you make it easier for yourself? The first and most important piece of advice has to be to learn the language. Any words you can learn before you move will help you a great deal. The second is to make some friends. Other immigrants are often the easiest to befriend and most supportive, simply because they will share your complaints and won't be hurt by your comments as the Swedes would. By all means, make some Swedish friends as well—but remember they are a reserved people, so don't feel hurt or discouraged if it takes you longer than expected. Finally, get busy! If you don't work, join local sports, crafts or educational groups. Lead a language course, play football with a local club. Sweden is the place to do it, Swedes love societies. The more involved you are the less you'll mind the differences, and you'll enjoy them instead.

The main key to surviving culture shock is preparation and understanding. Books like this one, and those listed in the back of the book, are there to help you. Remember to use Swedes as a resource—and make the most of your time in Sweden!

SWEDISH FOOD

CHAPTER 6

'Man tager vad man haver.'
('You take what you have.')
—Swedish proverb about food,
attributed to cookbook author Cajsa Warg

WHAT DO SWEDES EAT? Nowadays the meals are a similar multicultural mix as found in other Western countries: spaghetti, meatballs, tacos, fish, curries, etc. However, this is a fairly recent development and previously, the national diet relied very heavily on dairy products, pork products, fish, and root vegetables. This resulted in, among other delicacies, one of the most famous of Swedish meals, called the *smörgåsbord*.

SMÖRGÅSBORD

Anywhere you are in the world, you are likely to have heard of one Swedish meal: the *smörgåsbord*. This buffet meal actually means 'sandwich table', and is nowadays most often found in tourist areas or around Christmas time (when it is called a *julbord*, literally a Christmas table). Plates and plates of different herring and pork dishes, breads, potatoes, salads and cakes are laid out onto a long table for self service. Often the centrepiece is an entire decorated pig's head, and while a buffet is considered to be less formal in many countries, in Sweden an invitation to a *smörgåsbord* is an honour. It is a delicious meal, but not everyday eating in Sweden.

EVERYDAY FARE

Traditional Swedish meals are not unlike those in many northern European countries and are based on potatoes, meat and bread. Not very long ago, most meals consisted

Just a sample of the range of dishes served at a *julbord*, the Christmas version of the *smörgåsbord*.

of a little meat or fish, a lot of potatoes with some sauce and some bread on the side. Of course, this varied depending on the region. In the north, the meat was as likely to be game, whilst on the west coast, fish was eaten much more. The type of bread eaten also depended on the region; the everyday loaf, or *limpa*, seen everywhere now was only eaten in the south, where crops were better.

Swedish crispbread, or *knäckebröd*, comes from the middle regions of Sweden, where the flour could only be ground in the spring and autumn, when there was enough water to drive the mills. Because the flour would not keep for six months, the dry thin crispbread was the obvious answer. The northerners ate *tunnbröd*, or 'thin bread', which is not unlike a tortilla, because the only crop which would grow there, barley, will not rise and so yeast bread could not be baked. Today, all three breads, as well as many other types of loaves, are eaten all over Sweden.

As Sweden was, until quite recently, a very poor country, most people lived chiefly on herrings and potatoes. When they feasted, however, the pig provided the most popular meats, in hams, bacon, sausages and pork. Although today Swedes eat many different types of food, most of the traditional holiday meals still include meat or fish. Some foods considered typically Swedish by the Swedes include *falukorv*, a type of sausage (Swedes eat a lot of sausages), *surströmming* (fermented fish), *ostkaka* (cheesecake), *ugnspannkakor* (oven baked pancakes; with either a savoury or sweet filling or topping) and *ärtsoppa* (split pea soup). In addition there are many traditional meals, referred to as *husmanskost*.

Husmanskost

Husmanskost means 'everyday fare' but in common usage, it refers to more traditional Swedish meals which are still commonly served. These would not be the type of meals you would invite guests to eat with you, and it may not be easy to find them in a restaurant. Such meals include:

- *Köttbullar med lingon*, which is a dish of pork and beef meatballs with lingonberry sauce

- *Pytt i Panna*, which is a form of hash, with potatoes and pork fried together
- *Sjömansbiff*, or 'sailor's beef', a casserole with beef, onions and potatoes, cooked in beer
- *Kåldomar*, beef wrapped in cabbage leaves, which is in fact originally a Turkish dish, brought back to Sweden by King Charles XII in the 18th century, and thought of now as typically Swedish
- *Blodpudding*, which is very similar to the Scottish black pudding, a type of blood sausage
- *Nyponsoppa* or rosehip soup which is a sweet dessert soup that's very popular with children

On Thursdays, Swedes traditionally eat pea soup with pancakes for dessert. Long ago, before the Reformation, Swedes fasted on Fridays, and needed a substantial meal on Thursdays to tide them through. Dried yellow pea soup is extremely filling, and kept them going. With mustard, it tastes lovely, though it is not easy to get used to drinking the warm *punsch* (a sweet alcoholic drink) with it as the Swedes do. As recently as ten years ago, this was still a widespread practice, but nowadays is more historical among the younger generation.

Another traditional dish, more often seen at holidays, is called 'Jansson's Temptation' and is made with herrings, grated potatoes, cream and onions. It is often served on a buffet table, perhaps alongside a ham.

Anyone coming to Sweden from Britain will not be too surprised by the food, but anyone moving from Asia or southern Europe may find the food rather bland. A lot of the dishes rely on dairy products and sauces rather than spices, and many kinds of food are sweetened. Bread made with sugar in it is something of an acquired taste if you don't have a naturally sweet tooth.

However, if you don't enjoy sweet bread, you can do as many Swedes do and bake it yourself. A lot of Swedes do their own baking, cooking and even gathering of food—it fits in with their enjoyment of the simple life. You can, of course, buy bread and cakes, but many Swedes bake their own. The selection of ready-prepared meals in shops has improved markedly in the past ten years, and the average Swede is now switching from making their own foods to more often buying prepared foods. In the past, for example, most Swedes would still make their own jam, or meatballs, but now most buy it ready-made. This has become more prevalent as Swedish meals became more international. Swedes became accustomed to buying ready-made curry sauces and ravioli, for example, and then found it easier to buy more and more ready-made food altogether.

FISHING, HUNTING AND PICKING

Any country with a long coastline produces lots of anglers and Sweden is no exception. Hunting is also popular in Sweden, and many people enjoy providing their own fish and game for the table (strict laws do regulate this). It is easy for you to join in this even if you don't enjoy fishing or hunting; most Swedes join in the annual pilgrimage to the woods to pick mushrooms and berries all summer and autumn. It is very important, if you have never picked mushrooms before, to go with an expert; some mushrooms are poisonous and while you can (and perhaps ought to) buy a field guide, there

are stories every year of enthusiastic mushroom gatherers picking the wrong mushrooms. Most local communities have groups which go on day trips with an expert every weekend in the early autumn, which is an excellent way to learn about the different species. You can also learn different recipes through these groups, and some adult education centres offer evening classes on picking mushrooms.

Berries are less dangerous and probably everyone picks these—even in the cities it is possible to find thickets in the parks. Among the berries you can pick are wild strawberries (*smultron*), bilberries and lingonberries (similar to cranberry). In the northern half of Sweden you can also find Arctic cloudberries (*hjortonbär*), a golden berry which makes wonderful jam.

Seafood

Swedes have always eaten a lot of seafood, because it was plentiful and cheap. Now it is less plentiful and cheap, but you will find that many fish and shellfish considered delicacies elsewhere in the world are very common in Sweden. For example, caviar is sold everywhere, and

Cloudberries, known as *hjortonbär* in Swedish, are found in the northern part of Sweden and make for a delicious tasting jam.

one brand, Kalles Kaviar, which comes in tubes, is very common on Swedish breakfast tables. Better quality caviar, which comes in jars, is often served with toast or as an appetiser.

The cheapest fish of all, herring, is now becoming increasingly expensive due to overfishing. However, the *inlagd sill* (herring which is marinated to preserve it), sold in jars everywhere, is still a staple in many Swedish homes. It comes in different sauces, such as mustard, onion and curry, and is perfect with some potatoes, crispbread and salad. As it is eaten raw, it may not be to everyone's taste, but it is much better than some of the other 'special' forms of herring beloved to Swedes.

One of the most famous within Sweden is called *surströmming*, which is rotten herring. It is a speciality of the north, and derives from a time when people preserved herring in as little salt as possible (as salt was so expensive), which made the herring ferment. Nowadays, it is mostly eaten for tradition's sake, although there are those who claim to enjoy it. Most Swedes who live south of Norrland speak with awe of the dreadful smell which comes out of the tins which the *surströmming* is kept in, and haven't managed to eat it themselves. If you want to try different types of herring (except *surströmming*, which is unusual), the best thing to do is to order a herring plate, or *sillbricka* in a restaurant, or to find a real *smörgåsbord* where often many different types will be on offer.

Other Swedish favourites include smoked eel, *gravadlax* (salmon preserved in salt and dill) and smoked salmon. Indeed, any smoked or preserved fish is still very popular in Sweden.

With all this fish, certain sauces are very popular, including soured cream and *hovmästersås*, a mustard sauce. Dill is often served with herring and with potatoes, and is important in Swedish cooking.

Swedish Meats

If you are tired of fish, try some game. Reindeer, venison, elk and such birds as grouse are all popular within season, and many restaurants have special game menus during the autumn. These are often served with lingonberry sauce and, of course, potatoes. Occasionally you may find rotmos, a mixture of mashed root vegetables, instead of potatoes.

COFFEE AND TEA

Swedes drink the second highest amount of coffee per capita worldwide. They drink it in the morning, after lunch, in the afternoon, after dinner and in the evening. Most Swedes drink it black, and you may like to remind them you take milk or cream, if you do; otherwise your cup will be automatically filled up to the rim when you are drinking coffee with friends. Gevalia, a luxury coffee in some countries, is the coffee of choice in Sweden. Nowadays, most Swedes brew their coffee with a filter coffee maker, or a *cafetiere*, but older Swedes will still boil up coffee grounds to make a very strong brew. Coffee grounds sold in shops are specially marked if they are for boiling; you should avoid *kokkaffe* if you don't want to boil your coffee.

Nowadays more people are starting to drink tea than before, especially herbal teas, which are seen as healthy. Even Swedes who are keen coffee drinkers may drink tea with breakfast and you can certainly find most types in Sweden. Note that if you order it in a restaurant, it may be made with a teabag; not a surprise for a North American, but probably best avoided by anyone from a tea-drinking country. This teabag trend, however, is changing and tea bars are becoming more popular.

In the big cities in Sweden, there are many cafés which serve espresso, cappuccino, café au lait or different Brazilian, Kenyan or Tanzanian grinds. Even in smaller towns there will always be a few cafés, or *konditori*, where you can order a cup of coffee and a cake. Having a mid morning or afternoon coffee and cake is a very pleasant custom in Sweden, and there are many cakes, such as cinnamon buns, soft gingercake, sugarcake, *wienerbröd* (Danish pastry) and *mazarin* (Sweden's favourite pastry, an almond tart topped with icing) which are well worth trying. If you like cream you will appreciate Swedish cakes and pastries even more. Most cafés sell cakes to take home as well, and all will sell special cakes in different seasons. You will find saffron buns (*lussekatter*) in early December for Lucia Day, gingersnaps (*pepparkakor*) throughout the Christmas season, and *semlor* (rolls filled with marzipan and cream, sometimes served in a bowl of warm milk with cinnamon) between Christmas and Easter.

There are many outdoor cafés in Sweden which serve coffees and cakes.

EATING OUT

If you are out and about and need a snack which isn't sweet, try one of the *gatukök* (literally, 'street kitchen') about, which traditionally sells hot sausages with bread (like hotdogs) but, now, are as likely to sell hamburgers and kebabs as well. Even in winter, there is usually a queue at these stalls, which move about the streets depending on where the business is. If you are out late, you'll see many of them on the streets waiting for the revellers to come out from bars and pubs.

Eating out at a restaurant is common for the midday meal, and many Swedes do eat their midday meal out at restaurants near their place of work, and take advantage of the daily special, which usually includes a hot meal, salad, bread and butter, a soft drink or light beer and the essential coffee for around 70 kronor—a bargain in Sweden. Look out for these specials, called *Dagens rätt*; they are an excellent way to eat Swedish meals inexpensively. Note that service

International Fast Foods

Sweden does have its fair share of McDonald's, Burger Kings and Pizza Huts and similar other fast food restaurants, frequented mostly by younger people. They taste the same here as anywhere else, though the prices may surprise you.

in most restaurants is always included, and there is no need to add any extra tip.

Otherwise, Sweden does not have a restaurant culture as many countries do. When Swedes eat an evening meal out, it is more likely to be for a special occasion, rather than on a regular basis. Entertaining out at a restaurant is not unusual in a business context but very unusual amongst friends, unless it is a group of friends all paying for themselves. In spite of this, the larger cities do have a thriving restaurant trade, with assorted fine restaurants, a sprinkling of Michelin stars and famous chefs, and many international restaurants offering Indian, Thai, Italian and other types of foods. In addition, cafes offering both lunch and afternoon snacks are very popular.

FOOD SHOPPING

When you first shop for food in Sweden you may find it difficult to find the same goods on sale as at home. Sweden has long been a homogenous country, and it is only in the past 30 years that immigrants have brought in more exotic foods. However, you can find more and more international foods in larger supermarkets, especially in the cities.

In addition, there are many shops run by immigrants from Asia, especially China, and the Middle East, where you can find Asian, Middle Eastern and Indian foods, including inexpensive bulk bags of rice and even several types of British foods, like custard. Some smaller towns have these shops; otherwise you may like to make an occasional visit to Stockholm, Göteborg or Malmö to stock up. If you have space when you are moving to Sweden, it is worth bringing some of the more exotic ingredients you favour; and most foreigners in Sweden do seem to personally import their favourite foods whenever they go home for a visit.

Swedes shop for their food at supermarkets, though in many towns, fruit and vegetable stalls are a cheaper option

A table set with a typical midsummer buffet. Herring and new potatoes are the main components. Adjusting to a new diet can be difficult but Swedish food is generally healthy and tasty.

in the warmer months. These stalls are usually run by immigrants, and are a new thing for Sweden; not all towns do have them yet. Near a coastline, however, all towns have fish markets and stalls. Often these move about the town or city and will be in your neighbourhood one morning or afternoon a week (announced in advance). The fishermen occupy these stalls on a rota basis and, while they often can't speak English, they are as helpful as they can be with hand signals and a few words. Once you learn a little Swedish, they are extremely helpful and will tell you how to cook any of the fish they sell—important if you've never seen some of the North Sea or Baltic varieties before!

In some areas, it is possible to still shop at many small shops, a baker, a grocer, a butcher, a cheese shop and so on, but the supermarket is the most common place to do a large weekly shop. It is convenient and keeps longer opening hours, generally opening on Sundays as well. Shops such as ICA and Coop are all over Sweden, and are reasonably priced. There are usually a few very low priced shops as well; Willys and Lidl are popular discount supermarkets. All supermarkets provide plastic or paper bags, which you have to pay for. Some smaller shops don't, so remember to bring your own. All measurements are in metric, and by law there should always be a *jämförpris*, or comparison price, which allows you to compare prices per 100 g on every article.

Systembolaget

A very popular shop in Sweden is called Systembolaget, which is the only place that sells alcohol to take away. There are no other wine shops, off-licences, package stores or liquor stores and the state maintains a monopoly on the sale of alcohol.

In Two Minds

Swedes have mixed feelings about the monopoly. Many point out that the selection is excellent and the assistants are knowledgeable, and believe that the alcoholism problem in Sweden might get much worse if the monopoly disappeared. However, the restricted opening hours and the prices annoy Swedes too. The Systembolaget monopoly may end in any case, due to pressure from other members of the European Union; while anyone who lives in easy driving distance of Denmark will often buy all their alcohol there in preference.

In general, the most popular alcoholic drink is beer, which in Sweden is usually lager. This comes in four basic strengths: weak (Klass 1 or *lättöl*), which can also be bought in supermarkets and other shops; strong (Klass 3, or *starköl*) and two medium strengths (called *folköl* and *mellanöl*). Usually, *lättöl* is drunk like a soft drink, or if one is driving afterwards. Sweden has extremely strict drink driving laws, so if you are driving you should not order a *starköl*.

Beer Strengths

The strengths of the beers are 1.8 per cent, 2.8 per cent, 3.6 per cent and 4.5 per cent. In Sweden, these strengths are a measure of percentage by weight, so the 4.5 per cent strength of a *starköl* is equivalent to 5.4 per cent when measured by volume.

To buy *lättöl* or *folköl*, you must be at least 15 years old. You can buy these in supermarkets as well as Systembolaget. To buy anything from the Systembolaget (nicknamed just

Systemet), you need to be 20 years old. There is a definite love-hate relationship between Swedes and the Systemet. This has eased in recent years as Systemet has increased opening hours (10:00 am–6:00 pm on weekdays and 10:00 am–1:00 pm on Saturdays, though some shops have longer hours; see http://www.systembolaget.se for information about specific shops).

The main office publishes a quarterly guide to the drinks sold in Systembolagets nationwide, with prices and with a code number. Most, if not all, shops offer self-service so you can simply pick up what you want; but you can also use the guide to order any of the Systembolaget's collection into your local shop.

The assistants receive a lot of training regarding wines and spirits so if you ask them which wine you ought to serve with poached salmon, they can give you good advice. However, in practice, the queues are usually so long that you don't often see people spending more time there than they have to.

Most foreign alcoholic drinks are available in Systembolagets, but the prices are frighteningly high. Swedes who travel abroad import their full share of duty-free allowances. Wine and beer are not taxed as heavily as spirits, and they are not much more expensive than in other northern European countries. Drinks such as whisky, vodka and gin are taxed according to their strengths, not their prices, so that the tax on the cheapest blended bourbon will be similar to that on an expensive single malt scotch.

Wine is now more popular in Sweden than it was before, as most people have travelled abroad and due to the fact that it is now cheaper than before. However, traditionally and at formal parties, Swedes will always drink *snaps* of strong alcohols like *brännvin* and *besk*, which are flavoured shots of pure alcohol. Many Swedes distill these drinks at home, although it is illegal, simply because they have done it for generations. Home brewing of *lättöl* and wine is legal and popular.

Other popular drinks you may come across are *punsch*, which bears no resemblance to the English punch, but is instead a strong sweet liqueur made with arrak and drunk very cold with coffee after a meal or warm with pea soup on a Thursday evening and *glögg*, which is warm spiced wine served with raisins and almonds at Christmas time.

ALCOHOLISM

A word about alcoholism in Sweden: Swedes are not as used as many other Western cultures to drinking in moderation. They drink very little alcohol on a daily basis but do like to drink a lot when they are out on the town or at a party. Because of this, they have earned a reputation in many European resorts of being unable to handle alcohol, and if you see young rowdy Swedes staggering down the street at 3:00 am you may agree.

However, the alcohol problem is not really any worse than in most countries. It is sometimes more noticeable though because it is in such contrast to the general sobriety of the majority of Swedes. There are often a few people queueing outside the Systembolaget on a Friday morning (when the benefit money is paid out) and Swedes are very worried about alcoholism. This is part of the reason why the state monopoly has lasted so long and why many Swedes still support it.

SOCIAL DRINKING

If you go out drinking in the evening with Swedish friends, do not be surprised if they drink more than you would be comfortable with and, whatever you do, don't let yourself be pressured into drinking the kind of *snaps* and spirits that they like unless you do too. On the other side of the coin, if you are invited to a Swedish home for a casual meal, you are very likely to be offered cider, milk, orange or berry squash or Ramlösa water instead of a beer or wine. Wine and spirits, in particular, are reserved for parties or special occasions.

SVERIGE ÄR FANTASTISKT!

'... our land is big enough for the one who has a mind and
spirit great enough to fill the empty expanses, and with
great thoughts to populate the empty wilderness...'
—from Strindberg's *Gustav Adolf*

IF YOU ENJOY WALKING, HIKING OR CAMPING in the countryside, Sweden will be a wonderful destination for you. Even if you are not near any of the national parks, you can enjoy walking on open land because of the Swedish tradition of Allemänsrätten—'every man's right'. This allows everyone to enjoy the countryside, even if the land is private, within certain rules. Walking in fields and forests, picking flowers,

'Every man's right' means that Swedes are entitled to enjoy the countryside, as long as no damage is done. Here a Swede takes a break from walking on a trail in northern Sweden.

berries and mushrooms, and swimming and boating in lakes and the sea are all considered rights for everyone who lives in Sweden. It is important, however, to remember your obligations towards the land (and the people who may own it), so try to keep in mind the following rules when you venture out into the countryside.

Crossing Other People's Land

As long as you do not damage growing crops or seedlings, and do not trespass in someone else's private garden (the land immediately surrounding a private house), you can walk or ski on other people's land without having to seek permission from the owner of the property. If the land is fenced in, you can still go across, as long as you shut the gate properly behind you and do not damage the fencing. It is illegal to climb over any fence enclosing a private home.

There are certain exceptions to this rule. The military will restrict access to some areas for defence reasons, and you are not allowed to disturb any areas which are set aside for the protection of animals. These areas will be signposted. Any signs forbidding entry can only be put up with the permission of the local authority (except for the land immediately surrounding a house).

Camping

You may put up a tent and camp for a night or so if the land is not near a private house and is not being used for farming or cultivation of crops, and you don't need to ask the landowner's permission. For longer than a day, or if you are near a private house at all, you should ask permission, but few will refuse you unless you are likely to damage something. This is only for one tent—any groups who want to camp should always ask for permission.

Boating and Swimming

You are allowed to swim and also to moor your boat temporarily and go ashore at any point except at a private house or where the area is restricted for military purposes or to protect wildlife. You can row, sail, canoe or drive a motorboat in water which belongs to other people, but there may be special restrictions (such as speed limits or a ban on waterskiing).

Picking Berries and Plants

You may pick wild berries, flowers and mushrooms, and pick up fallen branches and dry wood. Some plants are protected because of their rarity, and you are not allowed to pick these (check with your local authority if you are not sure), nor are you allowed to take growing trees or bushes, bark, leaves, acorns, nuts or resin from growing trees. This is because it will damage the trees, and is considered to be theft. Taking a bird's nest or eggs is absolutely forbidden, and there is no 'every man's right' to hunt.

Making Fires

As long as you are sure that it is safe to do so, you are allowed to light a fire. It must be completely extinguished before you move on, and in certain areas, can be banned during times of drought. Fires are not allowed to be built on rockcliffs, as the cliffs might crack.

Taking Dogs Out in the Countryside

You can walk your dog freely in the countryside, but during the spring and the summer (between 1 March and 20 August), you must keep it on a lead. At all times, you need to make sure your dog is under control so that it won't scare or hurt any wildlife.

Clearing Up After Yourself

Whenever you have been out walking, boating, camping or otherwise enjoying the countryside, you must tidy up after yourself. This is simply good manners; do not leave rubbish lying about. You should not leave rubbish bags beside a rubbish bin when the bin is full because animals can easily tear them open and spread the rubbish around. It's easy for animals to injure themselves on cans, bottles, plastic bags or other pieces of rubbish.

> **Keep In Mind**
> The rules of 'every man's right' exist only to protect the land from any careless or foolish damage, and the rules come from basic common sense. Such a privilege carries responsibilities with it, and you must not abuse it.

THE OUTDOORS LIFE

Many favourite pastimes in Sweden centre around nature and the countryside. When I asked eight separate classes of English language students what they liked to do best on the weekends, the most common response was, "Go for a walk in the woods." Some of the other responses were very similar, such as jogging in the woods, berry or mushroom picking, or picnicking out in the country.

You can enjoy any of these pastimes on your own, or you may like to join one of the excursions and rambles organised by a local association or by the town's own recreation committee (*fritidsnämnden*). These committees are charged with ensuring that all who live in the town have an opportunity to enjoy outdoor (or indoor) recreation, and they work with many recreation centres and associations. Several such associations have united in the Swedish Guide and Scout Council (http://www.scout.se, but only in Swedish), and over 140,000 Swedish children join to camp and enjoy many other outdoor activities with them. Another organisation, for all ages, is Friluftsfrämjandet (open air supporters' group) (http://www.friluftsframjandet.se), which offers open-air schools for children and teenagers, and training courses for recreation leaders.

Many towns and cities have marked trails, suitable for walking, running and skiing, and sometimes also for cycling and horseback riding (details are often given in the local phone books). Many adult education centres offer courses in recognising edible mushrooms, so you can learn to enjoy fresh mushrooms safely. Other popular outdoor pursuits include gardening, camping and outdoor sports. Even aerobics and keeping fit turns into an outdoor sport in Sweden in the summer, with instructors setting up on platforms with boom boxes in the public parks.

Roughing It?

For many Swedes, camping is a fine art, supported by cars full of equipment and an extensive network of campgrounds. Many of these campgrounds have electricity hook-ups for caravans and a separate area for tents, and provide not only hot showers, toilet blocks, barbecues, picnic tables and a local emergency shop, but added extras such as washing machines and dryers, television rooms, mini-golf, tennis, boat hire and cafés. If you don't want to sleep in a tent or a caravan, you can rent a small cabin with running water and bunkbeds in many campgrounds. The idea behind all of these places is that you need a place to sleep and store your gear, but otherwise you will want to enjoy the fresh air for meals and all your recreation. Some of the campgrounds stay open all winter long—camping in the snow is not that unusual although the cabins may not be heated.

Hiking and Walking

These are popular pastimes throughout Sweden although the most challenging routes are in the northern national parks, especially Sarek, where only experienced hikers should go, ideally with a guide.

Swedish Tourist Foundation

There are many Swedish Tourist Foundation (STF, which stands for Svenska Turistforeningen) huts along routes, and you can stay a night there for a small fee. Get in touch with STF if you are interested in doing any hiking, as they can provide a lot of useful information on routes, places to stay and guided tours. They can be reached at tel: (08) 463-2100 and you can get more information on their website at:

http://www.svenskaturistforeningen.se/

Fishing

With over 96,000 lakes and a long coastline, fishing has always been popular in Sweden. Grilling your own freshly caught fish in the open air on a sunny Swedish evening will

certainly help you appreciate the native love of the countryside. For most fishing, you will need to buy a fishing permit, althoughthe coastline and some parts of Vänern, Vättern, Mälaren and other large lakes are considered to be open water. Many permits only cover fishing with a rod and reel, not with a net, and fishing from a boat is sometimes restricted.

Fishing Authorities

- Domänfiske is one authority which administers over 1,000 lakes and rivers and sells inexpensive permits for its own areas. You can buy these annually, weekly or daily. They publish brochures with more information, available directly from Domänfiske via their website, http://www.sveaskog.se, which also offers information on hunting.
- Contact your local tourist office or authority for information on any open water in your area.

Hunting

Hunting is even more restricted than fishing, but remains popular amongst many Swedes, particularly in the middle to northern region. You must own or lease land with hunting rights, and only hunt animals during their specific seasons. A hunting schedule (*jakttabell*) is published every year which gives details of the opening and closing days of a season for each animal. If an animal is not included in the hunting schedule, it is always illegal to hunt it. You can buy the schedule at most gunsmiths, sports shops and ironmongers or hardware stores. Note that if you want to buy (or own) a gun you must apply for a gun licence from the police; gun ownership is strictly controlled.

Skiing

Both cross-country and downhill skiing are extremely popular in Sweden, with excellent mountain resorts in the north and along the Norwegian border. Not many of these resorts are visited by non-Swedes but they are packed with school, work and family groups throughout the winter. Parts of southern Sweden see very little snow, particularly on the coast, so skiers travel even for cross-country trails. If you don't ski when you move to Sweden, you should certainly try it; it's one of the best ways to enjoy the coldest times of the year and, of course, it's outdoors. You can often borrow equipment from friends. Otherwise you will certainly be able to rent it at any resort.

For safety's sake, note that some mountainous areas are susceptible to avalanches. These are marked with yellow signs showing buried skiers. The risk is greater on steeper slopes, in new snow, in high winds and rising temperatures. Stick to the marked trails to be safer. Even if you are an experienced cross-country skiier, you should not leave the marked trails without a good map and equipment, and do check the daily forecast before you set out. Whether skiing or hiking, you should always make sure someone knows that you are going, and leave a copy of your route so that rescuers, if necessary, will know where to look for you.

Skiing is an activity that the whole family can enjoy together.

If you enjoy watching skiing, make your way to Mora for the Vasaloppet, the 90-km (56-mile) cross-country ski race commemorating Gustav Vasa's flight in 1523, which attracts thousands of participants. You can also enter if you enjoy a challenge but remember, it takes even the fastest up to four hours to complete. World Cup skiing is widely covered on Swedish television.

Boating

Sailing is one of Sweden's most popular sports, whether on the west coast, in the Stockholm archipelago or on the thousands of lakes. You can take sailing lessons or join a sailing club in many coastal towns, and many children enjoy messing about in dinghies during the warm summer months. If you already sail, it's worth meeting up with other sailors just to learn the Swedish sailing terminology, especially if you enjoy racing. Also, many clubs organise weekly competitions. Canoeing, rowing (both rowboats and racing shells) and motorboating are also popular, with kayaking a growing sport. Steamboats ply the Göta Canal from Göteborg to Stockholm in the summer.

With thousands of lakes and a long coastline, boating is a favourite pastime for many Swedes. These Swedes are journeying to a summer house on one of the Bohuslän islands.

If you plan to cruise around Sweden, you should buy a copy of Gästhamnsguiden, which gives details of nearly 500 guest harbours. Note that the 112 emergency services telephone number covers the sea rescue network as well. You can buy charts in many harbour sailing shops, or ask at tourist offices.

Cycling

Sweden is one of the countries where cycling is still a good alternative to driving, and many Swedes cycle to work or school, even in the winter, on the network of cycle paths. These are generally separated from streets for safety's sake, and the network can take you around the country as well with over 20 off-road and posted national routes, all with extra information available. The longest tour is Sverigeleden, which links many of the routes into one over 6,000 km (3,728 miles) long. Racing, touring and mountain bikes are all popular, and you should be able to find a new or used one within your price range.

Information on Cycle Paths

Cycle paths information is available from tourist offices.

Alternatively, you can look up Cykelfrämjandet's website at:

http://www.cykelframjandet.a.se.

However, as not much information is given in English, it might be easier to email them at:

cyklamera@cykelframjandet.a.se.

Cycle races are popular, and the longest one is Vättern Rundan, a 300-km (186-mile) race around the lake of Vättern in June. Again, this is only for experienced cyclists.

Orienteering

This cross-country race was invented by a Swede in 1918, and includes running a secret route with the help of a map and compass. It is based on military exercises and has become very popular in Sweden, with many meets and competitions staged in different areas throughout the late spring, summer and early autumn. The biggest meet is the five-day long O-Ringen, in July every year, where thousands compete in different age and ability classes. Like sailing or skiing, orienteering is a sport in which all family members can enjoy the outdoors and compete in friendly meets.

OTHER SPORTS

There are many other ways to enjoy being outside, but perhaps the most popular of all is through more sport. The Swedish Sports Federation estimates that almost half of the country's inhabitants are members of a sports club, and that two million people actively participate, either playing, coaching or supporting the club in some way.

Sports Celebrities

Swedes follow their national sides devotedly and if you live in Sweden for any length of time, you'll have much more to talk about if you can take an interest in their sports heroes. The three greatest heroes of the past are Björn Borg in tennis, Ingmar Stenmark in downhill skiing and Ingemar Johansson in boxing. Nowadays the Swedish football, ice hockey and handball teams are revered, as well as competitors in skiing, athletics and golf. Anyone with a Swedish connection is generally supported as much as a Swede.

Golf, tennis, football, ice hockey, table tennis and handball are amongst the sports where Swedes have excelled internationally; and whenever a Swedish team or athlete does well abroad, it boosts interest in the sport at home, as Christian Olsson and Carolina Kluft have done for athletics and Anja Pärsson for skiing.

Sports Clubs and Societies

It is said that when two Swedes meet they start a society, and the over 22,000 sports clubs in Sweden seem to bear this out. The Swedish Sports Confederation holds to the motto of 'Youth Sports and Sports for All' and more than 66 per cent of boys and 50 per cent of girls between the ages of 7–15 belong to a sports club. These clubs are the foundation of the sports movement in Sweden and rely heavily on the more than 500,000 Swedes who volunteer as leaders. The independent and democratic sports club system is a very

Swedes enjoy the outdoors, no matter what the weather. The sea moat behind this fort has frozen over so it's time to take advantage of a new place to skate and play ice hockey!

special one in Sweden, and underlines the Swedish love of consensus and cooperation.

In addition to the 67 specialised sports federations which make up the Swedish Sports Confederation, there are category federations such as the School Sports Federation, the Association for Company Sports (there are over 7,000 company sports clubs) and the Sports Organisation for the Disabled. According to the Confederation, the aim is to include old, young, able-bodied, disabled, men, women, Swedes, immigrants, carefree keep-fitters and almost fanatically serious elite athletes, and all spectrums between. Some federations are huge—the Swedish Football Association, for example, has 3,375 clubs—while others are much smaller.

If the sport you play is not represented locally, or if you just want to, you can start up your own club. There should be at least ten of you, and you should agree on what sports you want to concentrate on. The local authority can advise you as to where you can meet and train, and whether you are eligible to receive any financial grants. For a sport to actually join the Confederation, it must satisfy certain conditions: it must be non-profit; it must accord with the ideology and goals of the moment; it cannot be related to a sport already represented; it must be spread over at least half of the sports districts; and it must have at least 50 member clubs and 3,000 members.

Every student in any Swedish school studies sport and health as a separate subject in primary and secondary schools. In addition, public sports secondary schools, covering 32 sports, allow young athletes to study and train and compete with other young sportsmen and women. The largest of such schools train athletes in skiing, athletics, ice hockey, football and orienteering. Top sportsmen can choose to do their military service in a special sports platoon.

Sports Calendar

The biggest events in the Swedish sport year include competitions both in Sweden and abroad. The purely Swedish ones, however, are special to the Swedish heart. The calendar looks like this:

February/March

- World Cup Skiing at Lake Siljan

March

- Vasaloppet, the cross-country skiing race in Mora

May

- Göteborgsvarvet, a half marathon with over 35,000 participants

June

- Vätternrundan, the cycling tour around Lake Vättern
- SEO, the Swedish golf tournament, which moves to a different location each year
- Vansbro, a 3-km swimming race held in Dalarna

July

- DN-Galan, the athletics meet sponsored by Dagens Nyheter
- Gotland Runt, a sailing race around the island of Gotland

O-Ringen—the largest orienteering competition—attracts thousands of entrants every July. Many participants and spectators gather here around the finish line.

- Five-Day O-Ringen in orienteering
- Båstad Grand Prix tennis tournament

August
- Stockholm Marathon

August/September
- Finnkampen. The longest running track and field competition between two nations is in Sweden and Finland on alternate years, and is always sold out.
- Lidingöloppet, a 30-km road race

November
- Stockholm Open Tennis.

Anyone can compete in many of these events (except the elite competitions, such as World Cup skiing, Finnkampen and the golf and tennis events) but thousands watch them as well. If you can complete the Vasaloppet, Vätternrundan, Vansbro and Lidingöloppet in the same year, you have achieved a Klassikern. Amazingly, more people accomplish this every year.

NOT JUST SPORTS

Sports are a favourite amongst Swedes year round, but in a country with such different weather conditions during summer and winter, they naturally have different ways of spending their free time in the different seasons. You will find that Swedes take it easy in the summer, enjoying the outdoors and sports, and often retiring to small cottages by the sea, in the mountains or near lakes, where they can relax and forget about modern life.

In the winter, it's another story; while many sports are enjoyed year round, or even in winter only, Swedes have many other hobbies to take them through the long dark months. Many Swedes enjoy creating and fixing things to make their lives more pleasant and comfortable. Knitting and embroidery are popular, as are woodworking and painting. Swedes love to work on their homes, and practise DIY on everything from car repairs to home improvements. Some of the older crafts, such as candle-making, are popular in some areas. Home-baking and sewing are hobbies for some, while others consider them simply a part of everyday life.

SELF IMPROVEMENT AND ADULT EDUCATION

Swedes are fond of self improvement, and what better way to improve oneself than by attending a course? Adult education follows a long tradition of study circles in Sweden where traditionally, a group of people would get together to learn a craft, a language or an academic subject together. The leader is not considered a teacher, but simply further ahead than the others and therefore able to lead them.

Nowadays, formal classes, with a qualified teacher and a certificate at the end are as prevalent as study circles, particularly where the subject can be business related. In a class, the teacher will set the pace while the members of a study circle decide for themselves how quickly they want to learn and how much work they want to do (consensus again). Most study circles or evening classes meet once a week, in the evenings or on the weekends, and are a good way to get to know other people who share your interests. Subjects such as guitar playing, car maintenance and basketweaving tend to be less expensive than computer programming or navigation.

THE ARTS IN SWEDEN

The arts are as popular as sports amongst Swedes who are, in general, keen amateur singers, dancers and craftspeople. There are, of course, many professionals as well. In spite of their popularity at home, the arts and music of Sweden are little known in the rest of the world, beyond the pop group Abba, so popular in the 1970s, and the films of Ingmar Bergman, giving a fairly bleak view of Sweden. A few people may also know the playwright August Strindberg, the actress Greta Garbo, and perhaps the artist Carl Larsson. Sweden is a very small country, in population terms, and Swedish is a 'small' language with few speakers. Many talented filmmakers, writers and musical groups who are very popular at home find it difficult to break into the international arena, although more and more have done so recently as more artists record in English and writers and films are translated and dubbed into other languages.

Support for the Arts

The arts in Sweden are subsidised and supported by both the state and large corporations. The state funds grants to libraries, theatres, the opera and publishers, among others. Newspapers and magazines are also subsidised, as are specific art exhibitions and performances. To help everyone in such a 'spread-out' country enjoy the arts, the National Travelling Theatre (Riksteatern) performs all over the country in different towns and cities. For big international performances, you may have to travel to Stockholm, Göteborg or Malmö, but many of these will be sponsored for travel to smaller towns.

As well as this, every county has its own museum (*länsmuseum*) with arts and history from that region. There are many excellent museums in the larger cities, and the entrance fees are generally low because of state support. The national museums are in Stockholm, with the country's artistic, design and historical treasures, but there are many interesting museums in the other cities and throughout the countryside.

The biggest theatres and dance troupes are, again, in the big cities. However, many of the groups travel throughout the country, and amateur dramatics and dance are very popular. English-speaking theatre makes an appearance from time to time, either with visiting groups or local amateur theatre. Look out for special performances, such as *Hamlet* performed in a medieval castle, or the street theatre in Stockholm in the summer. If you are interested in participating, look online or in your local newspaper where many classes and amateur groups advertise. All different kinds of dance are popular in Sweden, though folk and ballroom dancing hold a special place in the Swedish heart.

Music

Part of the reason dance is popular is because Swedes are a very musical people. You can hear that in their accents when they speak! But joking apart, most Swedes enjoy singing, whether in an organised group, as a performer, or simply with friends at a celebratory party. One of the most famous Swedish singers was Jenny Lind, the opera singer called the 'Swedish Nightingale' who enchanted audiences internationally in the 19th century. She is honoured in Sweden with her picture on the 50-crown note.

Today, singing in a choir, religious or secular, is one of the most popular hobbies in Sweden. At parties, guests will often sing special songs for the occasion, beginning with children's songs at birthday parties, midsummer and Christmas, and reaching a height of merriment with the drinking songs (*snapsvisor*) sung to help glasses of strong alcohol down at adult parties. When attending a special occasion, such as a 50th birthday party or a wedding, it's common for Swedes to write a special song in honour of the celebrations. They'll sing it a cappella, or with a guitar or piano, and it becomes an integral part of celebrating. At any large party, the hosts are likely to have photocopied song sheets for their guests to sing along.

Although rock, pop and dance music are popular in Sweden, the old folk music played at midsummer and other summer holidays, has never lost its appeal for Swedes.

Folk Music

Folk music, like folk dancing, is important to Swedes. Every county and area has its own music and songs. Much of the music is based on the fiddle, and is meant for dancing. Several composers in the late 19th century were inspired by traditional Swedish folk music, among them Wilhelm Peterson-Berger and Hugo Alfvén. Their music plays on the national soul even today, truly a part of the Swedish psyche.

Music, singing and dancing remain popular to this day. Swedish dance-band music is heard everywhere and spans the generations. It is an acquired taste, and sounds not unlike the dance music popular in many countries in the 1950s. However, all types of music have their following in Sweden. Classical music is represented by several world-class symphonic orchestras, and there are regular jazz festivals throughout the country. Such groups as the Esbjorn Svensson Trio tour to great acclaim internationally.

Popular Music

In the past 30 years, the Swedish rock and pop groups have been immensely popular both at home and overseas. Abba

Traditional folk dance and folk music are important to the Swedes.

(made up of Anni-Frid, Benny, Björn and Agneta—hence the name) won the Eurovision Song Contest in 1974 with 'Waterloo' and went on to be one of the most popular groups ever. Like many Swedish groups, they had both Swedish and English versions of their songs. The groups of today tend to sing only in English, as they aim for a bigger market from the beginning. The success of groups such as Ace of Base, Roxette and The Cardigans has earned a great deal of money for the Swedish economy. Indeed, Ace of Base broke all of the records with their album, *Happy Nation*, which sold over 20 million copies worldwide—the biggest sales ever for a first album. The group is criticised for producing 'middle-of-the-road' pop music in Sweden but perhaps this is another case of cutting down tall poppies—nobody should be too successful! At home, groups such as Kent are enormously popular and there are hundreds of others who have not yet made it abroad but whom you will hear when you live in Sweden. Most recently, José González from Göteborg has made a breakthrough in the UK and the US.

Film

Amongst the most famous Swedes abroad must always be counted the actresses Ingrid Bergman and Greta Garbo, both famous in Hollywood films earlier this century. However, there are many other Swedes, both behind and in front of the camera, who have contributed to the international film industry.

Among the first were Mauritz Stiller and Victor Sjöström, both directors who went to Hollywood in the 1930s. They were followed by one of the greatest directors of all, Ingmar Bergman. His films tackle serious questions of existentialism, religion and conscience. Many of his films were produced in the 1950s and 1960s (he was born in 1918), but are still shown today, particularly his classics such as *The Seventh Seal* and *Through a Glass Darkly*. His last film, *Fanny and Alexander*, came out in 1982.

Although Bergman has not made a film since then, the story of his parents' early marriage, which he wrote as a book, was directed by the Danish film-maker Bille August and released as the film *The Best Intentions* (*Den Goda Viljan*) in 1992. The six-hour long film was shown on Swedish television, but a shortened version was released in the cinemas, and it won the Palme d'Or at the Cannes Film Festival. Bergman is unquestionably one of the greatest directors in the film world, but his work is not universally appreciated. Just because he is Swedish certainly doesn't mean that all Swedes enjoy his films. Nor is his work necessarily representative of Sweden. One of his films, made in the 1950s, was about free love in Sweden. Probably much of the international sex reputation Sweden has can be traced to this type of film.

Many other Swedish directors in the 1960s and 1970s (and today) enjoyed international acclaim. Vilgot Sjöman, Jan Troell and Bo Widerberg worked worldwide on feature films and documentaries.

Today's filmmakers include several who have been successful in Hollywood and others who have chosen to work in Sweden. The films *Show Me Love* and *Together* from director Lukas Moodysson have been hits outside Sweden. In the 1990s, films such as *What's Eating Gilbert Grape?* and *My Life as a Dog* brought acclaim to director Lasse Hallström, while Bo Widerberg's *Med Lust och Fagring Stor* was nominated for an Oscar in 1996. The English director Colin Nutley, who lives in Sweden, has created a series of popular films around the fictional village of Änglagård. Most recently, up and coming directors such as Kristina Humle and Maria Blom are creating new Swedish films, while the Beirut-born Swede Josef Fares has made popular films such as *Jalla! Jalla!* which show a more multicultural side of Sweden.

Foreign Films

Films from all over the world are enjoyed in Sweden, and you may find that many non-English-language films are released earlier in Sweden than in English-speaking countries. There seems to be more of a willingness to watch films from different cultures than in many English-speaking countries, though, of course, Hollywood films are extremely popular in Sweden as well.

Both films and videos in Sweden are shown in the original language, with subtitles (except for children's films), so you won't have to wait until you can speak Swedish to enjoy them. However, the Swedish film industry produces many entertaining films, and it's worth trying these out as soon as your language ability is up to it.

Censorship

There is some state censorship of the film industry, and there is also a rating system, primarily to help parents decide which films are suitable for their children. The ratings are 7, 11 and 15, and they refer to the ages under which children are not allowed to see the film without parental supervision. Films which show too much violence can be censored, or given a higher rating. Unlike in the USA, where violence is rarely considered objectionable but sex is often censored, the Swedish authorities feel that it's less important to censor sex scenes than violence.

Television and Radio

As with film, so it is with television—a lot of imported programmes are shown in the original language, with Swedish subtitles. There are two main Swedish television channels (SvT1 and SvT2) which are non-commercial. Everyone with a television set pays a licence fee to the state-run Swedish Broadcasting Corporation to support these two channels and Swedish radio. Channels 1 and 2 emphasise cultural, news and educational programming, and the mix of documentaries, live opera and news programmes is sometimes criticised as being too serious and heavy. The standard, however, is generally high, and popular programmes from the US, UK and other Scandinavian countries are often broadcast. The most widely available commercial channel is TV4. Another commercial station, TV3, is less widely available although city dwellers should have no problem receiving it. There is no analogue television in Sweden and to receive television broadcasts you will need either a cable television subscription, a set top digital box or a satellite dish.

Pay Channels

Most Swedes today already subscribe to pay television, available either through a cable or through a satellite dish on the roof or in the garden. A basic menu of pay channels is likely to include a selection of English-language news and sports channels. You needn't be without such channels as CNN, BBC Prime, Discovery, Nickelodeon or many others, all available in Sweden. Many Swedes watch these programmes as a way of learning what is current in other countries.

Swedish radio offers several alternatives, with programmes in all of the major immigrant languages. Radio Sweden, at 7.38 mHz, broadcasts both international and Swedish news regularly in English. It also offers other English language programmes about Sweden—interesting to listen to if you want to learn more about current events and happenings in Sweden. You can also listen online wherever you are visiting their website at http://www.sr.se/rs/english. Several local stations also offer programming in English—check your local paper to see when. The number of commercial stations is growing. In or near a city, it is possible to listen to many different types of music and talk programmes.

The Press

Many Swedes prefer to turn to a mix of newspapers and television for their information. Among the largest national newspapers are *Expressen* and *Aftonbladet* (tabloid style newspapers), *Dagens Nyheter* (considered to be an independent liberal broadsheet) and *Svenska Dagbladet* (considered to be a conservative broadsheet). Two other newspapers, *Göteborgs Posten* and *Sydsvenska Dagbladet* are specific to the Göteborg and Malmö regions. In addition, the free newspaper *Metro* has a very large circulation and has local editions for the cities. In the past, most newspapers were affiliated with political parties, and so had a specific political slant; today, this still holds true of some. Most newspapers have Internet sites.

> Sweden has taken to the Internet culture faster than most non-English-speaking countries and there is a wealth of websites available, including many with governmental information. The country abbreviation is '.se'.

Freedom of the Press

All newspapers and other press are protected by the Freedom of the Press Act of 1975, which ensures that journalists have the right to protect anonymous sources and have free access to public documents. The Act also establishes procedures for trials concerning freedom of the press, which make it difficult to win financial judgments against journalists. In addition, a special *ombudsman* governs the press.

Magazines

There are many weekly, monthly and quarterly magazines and journals in Swedish, but many Swedes also read foreign magazines. English-language magazines are commonplace in any city, and will probably be available in the libraries of even quite small towns. The same is true of English-language newspapers, although since many of these are available online, it is not easy to buy these in Sweden any longer.

Books and Literature

In addition to being avid newspaper and magazine readers, Swedes buy more books per capita than any other European country. This is in addition to well-funded and utilised libraries. Compulsory education and the long winter evenings have combined to make reading a popular hobby throughout the country. For those who cannot get to their local library, there is a system of book-buses and book-boats. These follow a weekly route and it's possible to both borrow books from them and order specific books in advance.

Many Swedes buy books from special book clubs through the post. They sometimes specialise in certain subjects, and there are several clubs that offer English-language books. Bestsellers in English-speaking countries are often popular in Sweden, and many Swedes choose to buy these books in their original languages. For a foreigner or a recent immigrant, however, buying Swedish literature in English translation is not always as easy.

Swedes are avid readers, whether the material is a newspaper, magazine or book.

Nobel Prize Winners

There are many Swedish Nobel laureates in literature, but perhaps only two of these, Selma Lagerlöf and Pär Lagerkvist are well known outside Sweden. Lagerlöf, who won the Prize in 1909, also wrote popular children's tales. The literary trend of the late 19th century celebrated Swedish history and culture; Lagerlöf and other authors depicted the agrarian lifestyle of days gone by in idylls which were meant to represent the ideal Swedish lifestyle. This trend was mirrored in musical and artistic creations of the time.

By the early 20th century, during Pär Lagerkvist's (Nobel Prize Laureate in 1951) time, the climate was less positive. His works focus on the themes of existentialism and the struggle between good and evil, with *The Sibyl* and *Barabbas* among his best known works.

Other Literary Figures

The works of well-known author and playwright August Strindberg (1849–1912) are widely available in English. Plays such as *The Father* and *Miss Julie* are performed worldwide. Both Lagerkvist's and Strindberg's works offer an often desperate and bleak view of life; though this ought not to be taken as a general reflection of Swedes!

Proletarian literature first became popular in the 1930s. Authors such as Ivar-Lo Johansson and Harry Martinson wrote about the working classes, often with the theme of social injustice, giving an excellent depiction of their lives of hard work and poverty in the 19th and early 20th centuries. The works of the best-known author of this genre, Vilhelm Moberg (1898–1973), are available in English and have been made into films starring Max von Sydow (another famous Swedish actor) and Liv Ullman. The quartet of books, *The Emigrants*, *The Immigrants*, *The Settlers* and *The Last Letter Home*, tell the story of an impoverished Swedish family's immigration to America.

Few recent Swedish books are available in English. Some authors to look out for are Jan Myrdal, a talented documentarist with sometimes controversial political ideas, and Kerstin Ekman, Sven Delblanc and Jan Guillou, all popular novelists with very different styles.

In the 1990s, a new interest in Scandinavian literature in the English-speaking world awoke, with Peter Høeg of Denmark (author of *Miss Smilla's Feeling for Snow*) and Jostein Gaarder of Norway (author of *Sophie's World*) paving the way. More of Kerstin Ekman's works have been recently made available in English, and the works of Henning Mankell have become so popular in English that many of his older works have now been translated as well. Another author to look out for is Marianne Fredriksson, while Mikael Niemi's *Popular Music from Vittula* is a recent bestseller which gives a taste of Finnish-Swedish life in the far north. Finally, such books as Jonas Hassan Khemiri's *One Eye Red* give an idea of the new immigrant literature just starting to be published in Sweden.

Fortunately, many children's authors have been translated, giving English-speaking children access to the works of Elsa Beskow, Astrid Lindgren's *Pippi Longstocking* and *Emil*, and Selma Lagerlöf's wonderfully adventurous Nils. If you have children, these books are a great way to introduce them to some of their new playmates' favourite characters (there are also many spin-off television programmes). Astrid Lindgren's books are considered by many to be part of Sweden's national treasure. Indeed, during Lindgren's funeral ceremonies, the whole of Sweden mourned and many took to the the streets of Stockholm to pay their last respects to the beloved author.

Design and Architecture

Throughout its history, functionalism has been important for Swedes, but everyday objects should also look good. The sleek lines of a Saab car, the clean medicine-bottle shape of an Absolut Vodka bottle, are part of the functionality of these useful things. Swedes appreciate simplicity, and much of Swedish (and Scandinavian) design is very sophisticated in its minimalism.

Modern architecture has benefited from functional concepts, although the popularity of the traditional little

Although functionalism is important in Swedish architecture and design, there have been occasions when this has given way to indulgence as seen in this exquisite interior of the City Hall (Stadshuset). The walls have been hand-gilded with more than 18 million gold-leaf mosaic pieces.

The red house is still an architectural icon in Sweden.

red house remains strong as well. Amongst the innovators in modern architecture have been Gunnar Asplund and Ivar Tengbom, who both worked in the early 20th century. Their designs for community buildings, such as libraries and concert halls, were based on the ideals of functionalism and simplicity.

Art

In addition to an appreciation for handicrafts and good design, Swedes appreciate fine arts, with painting and sculpture having a special popularity amongst Swedish artists. Visiting art galleries and collecting works of art at auctions is fashionable in the larger cities; anywhere in Sweden, you are more likely to find an original painting on the wall than a reproduction, and art appreciation evening classes are popular.

Swedish artistic trends were heavily influenced by European trends throughout the Middle Ages and Renaissance, with ornate wall painting, murals and decorations giving way

Kalmar Castle is an excellent example of Swedish medieval decoration.

to portraiture in the late 15th and early 16th centuries. The baroque and rococo styles popular in Europe in the 16th and 17th centuries influenced the Gustavian period of the 18th century. The Gustavian style, also called Swedish Neo-Classicism, is growing in popularity again today, with ornate furniture and decorations in simple surroundings and colours, reminiscent of Greek and Roman antiquity.

By the 19th century, artists were inspired by a more defined Nordic style, with classical and romantic painters choosing Norse mythology and Swedish history as subjects. By the late 19th and early 20th century, the national trend towards romanticism fostered a return to simplicity in the arts. Sculptors such as Carl Milles and Stig Blomberg and painters such as Carl Larsson, Bruno Liljefors and Anders Zorn all flourished at this time.

Anders Zorn is considered one of the most gifted Swedish painters but Carl Larsson also deserves a special mention. His watercolours and bright illustrations depict a romantic view of everyday life in the Swedish countryside. Larsson's work is still popular today, perhaps more so than 20 years ago, as many Swedes idealise the simplicity of the agrarian lifestyle of days gone by.

Modern Art

In the 20th century, artistic trends ranging from Cubism and Surrealism to Neo-Realism and Primitivism have all been represented in Sweden as they have throughout Europe. As in other countries, many younger artists prefer to concentrate on graphic and industrial design rather than classical painting and sculpture. However, state support means that new art, some traditional and some very experimental, is bought and displayed in public buildings (such as galleries and libraries). It's not all equally appreciated by the public, but ensures that the fine arts, from folk art and impressionism to modern and graphical art, remain very much a part of Swedish life.

Crafts

The love of functional uncluttered good design extends to many other arts and crafts popular in Sweden. Several of these, notably ceramics, glass and textiles, have grown into large industries with well established overseas markets.

Sturdy pottery looks wonderful and is popular, but the fine porcelain made by companies such as Rörstrand and Gustavsberg matches any made by other fine china-makers. Textile companies tend to concentrate on luxury fabrics and the traditional woven cloths of Sweden are beautifully designed and created.

Meanwhile, the great glass-blowing companies of Småland, such as Kosta Boda and Orrefors, create both luxury and everyday glass items for the world market. Glass-blowing came to Sweden with a Venetian and has been an important industry ever since. Many of the styles remain the same as they were a hundred years ago, with cut crystal and simple straight lines equally popular. However, the glass companies employ many younger designers who create beautiful, colourful and modern designs that are both functional and decorative. You don't have to go to Småland to see glass-blowing or buy original works; there are many smaller glass-blowers throughout the country and the beautiful glass is on sale throughout Sweden.

Many of the old-fashioned crafts which are less common in other countries are still popular in Sweden. Back in the 1950s, an English visitor observed, "In most countries, the magic of the all-powerful machine rapidly drove ancient handicraft traditions beyond recall. Sweden, however, was luckier. Here, the indigenous peasant craft was rescued in the very nick of time, just as it was on the brink of disappearing forever. Thus the people never quite lost their century-old designs, nor the feel of raw material in their hands." (*The Charm of Sweden*, 1956).

Swedish children learn handicrafts in school and knitting, embroidery, and woodcarving remain hobbies for many into adult life. Less common, but with a large following, are the crafts of weaving, lace-making, rug-making, candle-making and smithery.

Buying Handicrafts

Those who don't enjoy such crafts appreciate being able to buy handmade items. You can, of course, always buy cheap imitations made abroad. In spite of the expense, however, many Swedes prefer to buy the real hand-made and carefully designed goods.

If you get a chance, do travel to the Glasriket area of Sweden, near Växjö in Småland, where you can visit many of the most famous glassmakers, such as Kosta Boda, or Orrefors and buy first or second quality goods. Wine glasses, vases, plates and bowls or sculptures are all available; not much of it is cheap but it is all beautiful.

If you prefer wooden handicrafts, you might choose between a hand-painted Dala horse, a butter knife, or a cheese/sandwich board. The horse, which comes in many sizes, has almost come to be a symbol of Sweden, although in fact it is only made in the region of Dalarna. The knives and boards are still widely used in Sweden.

Other typically Swedish goods are ceramics, silverware and amber jewellery, pewter (especially made up in classic Viking designs), Sami handicrafts and textiles. A *toarpkronan*, which is an iron chandelier decorated with flags and ribbons, is often found in Swedish homes and makes

A symbol of Sweden, the Dala horse is a brightly-painted wooden carving of a horse.

a very unusual and lovely gift. The national handicrafts organisation, Svenska Hemslöjdsföreningarnas Riksförbund, endorses certain examples of Swedish crafts; these are marked with a round sticker with the words 'Svensk slöjd' on it.

The Jokkmokk market, in far northern Sweden, is held in February every year and if you can manage to get up to Jokkmokk you will have the opportunity to buy many authentic Sami handcrafts and foods. If you buy Sami handicrafts elsewhere, look out for the 'Duodji' label which is a mark of its authenticity.

A LITTLE TRAVEL

Of course, if you are able to take some time to travel, even if you aren't interested in buying glass in the Glasriket or Sami handicrafts in Jokkmokk, you'll be participating in another Swedish favourite leisure pursuit. Swedes travel a lot for pleasure, both at home and internationally.

Stockholm is a natural first stop; the nation's capital offers beautiful scenery, interesting museums, the royal palace, and even inner city fishing and boating, as well as innovative shops and restaurants. Children will enjoy Junibacken, a living fairy tale museum, while a walk around the Old Town (Gamla Stan) will entrance the adults.

The island of Gotland, off the east coast in the Baltic Sea, is worth a visit for a summer holiday, with wonderful beaches, the medieval town of Visby and old Viking runestones. Camping and cycling holidays are popular here; and many people rent tandem bicycles with camping trailers after them. Of course you can bring your car over on the ferry if you prefer.

The cities of Göteborg and Malmö have much to offer as the second and third cities. Göteborg's Liseberg amusement park and Universeum science museum are the two most visited tourist attractions in Sweden. Other popular areas for Swedes to visit include the rocky coasts of Bohuslän, especially for sailors; the skiing resorts of the Swedish mountains; the trip along the Göta Canal between Göteborg and Stockholm, and the

A view of Gamla Stan, or the Old Town. As the name suggests, this is the oldest part of Stockholm and dates back to the 13th century. A walk around the town will uncover many cobblestoned streets, ancient alleyways and impressive architecture.

"You Must Visit This Place!"

Many Swedes have a special connection back to their grandparents' or great-grandparents' county, perhaps because of a summer house, and so most Swedes will be able to tell you about their favourite and 'most beautiful' place which you must not miss.

university towns of Uppsala and Lund with their history.

While outside pursuits, sports and the arts are popular year round, Swedes love to celebrate the different parts of the year. In spite of increased diversity in the country, most Swedes still celebrate the same way throughout the year.

A YEAR IN SWEDEN

Calendar of Festivals and Holidays

Public holidays in Sweden are sometimes called 'Sundays' to confirm that they are not ordinary working days.

13 December	Saint Lucia Day
	(Not a public holiday but the beginning of the Christmas season)
24 December	Christmas Eve (Julafton)
	(When Swedes celebrate Christmas)
25 December	Christmas Day
	(A public holiday)
26 December	Annandag Jul (like British Boxing Day)
	(A public holiday)
1 January	New Year's Day
	(A public holiday)
6 January	Epiphany
	(A public holiday)
13 January	Trettondag Knut
	(Not a public holiday but the day Swedes take down their Christmas decorations)
February	Winter school holidays; referred to as Sportlov as many take the opportunity to go skiing
February/March	Shrove Tuesday
	(The last Tuesday before Lent, when Swedes eat special buns called *semlor*)

(Continued on the next page)

(Continued from previous page)

March/April	Good Friday, Easter Sunday and Easter Monday (As Friday and Monday are public holidays, schools take a week off)
25 March	Waffle Day (Our Lady Day, when Swedes eat waffles)
30 April	Walpurgis Night (Not a public holiday)
1 May	International Labour Day (A public holiday with many parades)
May	Ascension Day (A public holiday; a Thursday six weeks after Easter)
May/June	Whitsun (Not a public holiday; about ten days after Ascension Day)
6 June	Swedish Flag Day (A public holiday from 2005)
Third week of June	Schools break up for the summer
24 June	Midsummer Day (A public holiday, but is celebrated on the Saturday closest to the 24 June; most Swedes take Midsummer's Eve off as well)
July	Many Swedes take three or four weeks' holiday in July
August	Time to celebrate crayfish coming in season, with crayfish parties
1 November	All Saints Day (A public holiday, celebrated on the Saturday closest to 1 November)
10 November	Saint Martin's Day (Not a public holiday, but a day to eat goose which are now at their best)
End November	First Sunday in Advent (Four Sundays before Christmas, and time to start thinking about celebrating again)

Festivals and Holidays

Traditionally, the year in Sweden revolved around the Church year. Although not many Swedes are devout churchgoers now, most of the important Church festivals are still observed and many are public holidays.

The Church year begins with Advent, which starts on the fourth Sunday before Christmas. On the first Sunday in Advent, many Swedes go to church and get together for a meal afterwards or in the evening. It is the beginning of the Christmas season, and people start to think about buying presents, planning parties and decorating their homes. Decorations will already have gone up in the shopping centres (probably by early November, in fact). December is dominated by Christmas and also by Lucia Day. On children's television and radio there is a *julkalender*, which has a special show for each day in December leading up to Christmas, and many children open Advent calendars—coloured paper pictures which have small windows to open for each day from the 1st to the 24th. Behind each window is another picture, or a small present or chocolate.

Lucia Day

On 13 December, Sweden celebrates Lucia Day. The day is traditionally in honour of Saint Lucia from Sicily, but the day's celebrations today have little to do with her or any religious observance. There are three levels of celebration in most places. In many families, the youngest daughter (or child) dresses up as Lucia, with a long white robe and a wreath of candles on her head, and wakes her family up with the song 'Sankta Lucia' and coffee and saffron buns (*lussekatter*, specially made for Lucia Day), very early in the morning.

Unfortunately, this is less common today as everyone is rushing to get to school and work, but many people will still celebrate at school or their office. In many offices, the employees will start the day with coffee, saffron buns and gingersnaps (*pepparkakor*), or at least have it with their coffee break. Schools will often pick a Lucia and attendants and have their own small celebration, either first thing in the morning or in the evening. The Lucias can have as many female attendants (called *Luciatärnor*) and male attendants (called *stjärngossar*, or star boys) as they like, so all students can take part.

Finally, Lucia is celebrated on a local and national level as every local newspaper will have a competition to pick a Lucia for the town that year. These Lucias will usually lead a parade through town, and then spend much time during the Christmas season bringing saffron buns and gingersnaps to homes for the elderly and hospitals. Most of these Lucias are in their late teens or early twenties and invariably have long hair, though recently they are no longer always blondes. There is also an official Lucia for Sweden and many unofficial television Lucias, often filmed waking up famous people. It is a fun festival welcomed by everyone as a way of bringing light to a very dark time of the year.

Christmas

After Lucia, the country really gears itself up for Christmas, and most homes put up decorations including an Advent star (a large six-pointed star with a light in the middle) and

Children dressed up as Lucias, Christmas elves and gingerbread men for the Lucia Day party..

an electric candelabra in the window to light up the night. Many people change their curtains and put out a myriad of other decorations as well, and put up a Christmas tree in the week before Christmas. You can buy an artificial tree but most families buy a real tree, cut down specially for Christmas. In December, they are sold on many street corners so they are not difficult to find. Other popular Christmas plants are red poinsettias, tulips and begonias, as well as white, blue and pink hyacinths. It is common to send Christmas cards (often postcards) to friends and relatives in time for Christmas, especially if you will not see them, and to exchange gifts with relatives. Preparations for Christmas also include lots of cooking and baking, making of gingerbread houses and tree decorations, wrapping of presents, and, finally, travelling to relatives' homes to celebrate with them.

The actual festival begins at lunchtime on the 24th. Most workplaces and shops will close on the evening of the 23rd, and children finish school the week before for a two-week holiday. Many Swedes eat a traditional light meal of broth and bread for lunch and then settle down in front of the television to watch an omnibus edition of Disney cartoons for a few hours. This programme has been on the television for years and repeats every Christmas Eve.

In the evening, many families dress up and the real celebrations begin, with a big *julbord* (Christmas buffet table) of traditional Christmas foods, including several types of herring salads, liver paste, smoked sausages, a large ham and *lutfisk*—a dried fish marinated in lye and served with a white sauce or butter. Afterwards, rice pudding with either cinnamon or jam is served. An almond is hidden in the pudding and in some households, whoever finds it has to say a rice pudding rhyme The traditions vary from region to region. For example, in some homes, it is believed that the almond finder will be the next person to get married.

Just before or after dinner, the *jultomten* (literally, 'Christmas gnome', but actually a Father Christmas/Santa Claus figure) comes in with his red hat and white beard (but a red robe rather than suit) to distribute presents from a sack on his back. Unlike Santa Claus, however, the *jultomten* comes in through the door (the fireplace, if there is one, probably has a fire in it!) and asks directly, "Are there any good children here?" Christmas presents in Sweden are called *julklapp*, or 'Christmas tap', a tradition from the Middle Ages when people would sneak up to houses, tap on the door and quickly put a present inside and run away. Family members will also give presents to each other, and these are often put underneath the tree until Christmas Eve.

On Christmas Day, many go to an early morning church service, called *jullottan*, which often starts at 7:00 am and ends before dawn. It is a beautiful candlelit service with much singing, and is popular with churchgoers and non-churchgoers alike. After the service, it is time to eat some more, enjoy the new presents and the time together with family. The day after Christmas is a public holiday, and many Swedes have time off to spend with their families, and go skiing (if there is snow so early) and celebrate.

New Year

As in many countries, New Year's Eve is greatly celebrated with parties, champagne and fireworks throughout Sweden. Christmas food is still served, but the parties are now more for friends than for families. Every year on television, there is a repeat of 'The Duchess and the Butler', a little known English television sketch which many Swedes know by heart and, just before midnight, a reading of Alfred Tennyson's 'New Year's Clock' (in Swedish) which ends just as the clock starts to strike 12. In the cities, lots of people go out to watch the fireworks, in spite of freezing temperatures, and go on eating, drinking and dancing into the small hours, knowing that they can sleep in on New Year's Day.

Three Kings Day and the End of Christmas

But the Christmas/New Year holidays are not over yet. There is another holiday on 6 January, Epiphany, when the three wise men reached Bethlehem and it is called Trettondagen (Thirteenth Day) or Heliga tre konungars dag (Three Kings Day). In most countries, it is the day to take down the Christmas decorations but in Sweden, they are left up for another week, only to come down on 13 January, or Tjugondag Knut (20th Day Knut). This may be for several reasons; Swedes joke it is because they like Christmas more than other nations, and that they have such dark nights they need the Christmas lights, but it is more likely because the Vikings held a mid-winter feast on this day, and the early Church in Sweden tried to stop the pagan festivities by making 13 January part of Christmas. In any case, this is the day to take down all of the decorations and clean up after the festivities. A *julgransplundring* party, when the tree is stripped of its decorations and the last of the Christmas food is eaten up, is common amongst Swedes, especially for children, and is a good way to make a tiring task fun.

Sportlov (The Sports Holiday)

The next big holiday for children (and for all adults with children) is the school break in February, which is a wintersports holiday. Many families do go skiing in this week, although you have to book early for the popular ski resorts in Sweden and in the Alps. It is becoming more common to go to a warm climate for this week, as well. The weeks are staggered for different regions throughout Sweden, so that not every schoolchild is free during the same week, although Swedish ski resorts are still crowded during most of February.

Fastlag (Shrove Tuesday)

The six weeks before Easter (in late March or April) were traditionally weeks to avoid meat and fats, and so the last day before Lent begins, which is always on a Wednesday, is called Fat Tuesday in many countries. In Sweden, it is a day to eat *semlor*, buns which are filled with marzipan and whipped cream (also called *fettisbullar* and *fastlagsbullar*) which were traditionally served in a bowl of warm milk with cinnamon. Now many eat them as they are, and they are available right up until Easter, thus defeating the original object of eating up the fat in the house! Not many Swedes hold to the Lenten fast any longer and they prefer to enjoy *semlor* for as long as possible.

Waffle Day

Not a proper holiday, but many Swedes do still eat waffles on 25 March. The reason is not religious or traditional, but only because this is the Day of the Virgin Mary in the Church, which in Swedish is called Vår Fru Dag (literally, 'Our Lady Day') and the faster one says 'Vår Fru', the more it sounds like 'Våffel', or waffle—a good excuse to eat waffles in schools and many homes!

Easter

Easter, the holiest festival in the Church year, means a four-day break for most Swedes and two weeks for schoolchildren, during the time of year when the country is just coming out of winter. Again, many Swedes decorate their homes, changing to yellow or pink curtains and tablecloths, and putting birch twigs with brightly coloured feathers tied to them (called *påskris*) around their homes. Daffodils (called Easter lilies in Sweden) and tulips in pastel colours are also popular, and it is often time for a thorough spring cleaning before the family comes to visit for Easter.

A family celebrating a more traditional Easter would have an Easter dinner of eggs and lamb on Saturday evening (the day before Easter) after having eaten fish on Good Friday. Any small girls in the house will dress up as brightly coloured witches, with head shawls and long skirts, and will go around to the neighbours asking for Easter treats (usually chocolates, sweets or small change). Witches are not associated with Easter in many other countries, but in Sweden, the association comes from an ancient belief that during Easter, the witches went to visit the devil at Blåkulla and it was important to keep them from coming near one's own house whilst on their journeys. In some parts of Sweden, people light bonfires on Easter Saturday to keep the witches away. Swedes also enjoy eating Easter chocolates and sweets, and painting eggshells in bright colours for decorations. However, for most Swedes, these festivities are only a part of Easter. The four-day break from work is well timed to do a lot of early spring gardening, to begin to get the boat ready for the summer season, or to open up the summer

These young ladies are all dressed up for Easter.

house for the first time in the year. Still other Swedes take the opportunity to get in some of the last skiing of the year or to go abroad for a holiday.

Valborgmässoafton (Walpurgis Night)

Soon after Easter comes 30 April, when people get together in crowds to sing and have large bonfires. This is not a public holiday, but is the evening before the first day of May, which is one, so that Swedes know they can stay out late and sleep in the next day. The bonfires are again to frighten off witches and evil spirits going to visit the devil and are more common in Stockholm and the east than on the west coast where bonfires are more common at Easter. The holiday traditions are mixed together with traditional student celebrations of the beginning of spring on 1 May, common in Uppsala and Lund.

In Göteborg, the Chalmers University students put on a well-known parade with lots of floats and funny costumes; a very popular way to spend the early evening for both young and old. Many students and former students wear the white caps they earned by completing *gymnasium* on 30 April.

May Days

Traditionally the first day of May was the beginning of spring and was therefore a day off, but since the late 19th century, the gatherings in parks and city centres have been to mark International Labour Day, when many of the unions and workers march in the streets to commemorate workers' rights. They are joined by bands, orchestras and politicians giving speeches. Further public holidays in May are Ascension Day, the day in the Church calendar when Christ ascended into heaven (Kristi himmelsfärds dag), which is five and a half weeks after Easter, and always on a Thursday.

Whitsunday and Whitmonday (Pingstdagen and Annandag Pingst) are celebrated a week and a half after Ascension Day. Because Ascension Day is on a Thursday, many Swedes take the Friday off as well for a long weekend of gardening, sailing or just relaxing at their summer houses. The weekend of Whitsunday, on the other hand, is a traditional time for weddings, although Whitmonday is no longer a public holiday. The last Sunday in May is Mother's Day, when mothers and grandmothers receive cards, flowers and sometimes presents or chocolates from their families.

Flag Day

For a long time, Sweden had no national day until, during World War I, some Swedes began to privately celebrate the Swedish flag day on 6 June, which was the anniversary of the day that Gustav Vasa was chosen as the first Swedish king in 1523, and also of the day that one of the Swedish constitutions was signed in 1809. From 1916, more and more Swedes began to observe the day with parades and public gatherings, and it became a public holiday in 2005. The flag day was officially named the national day in 1983.

The End of the School Year

In many nations, the end of the school year is merely a relief for students and teachers, but in Sweden, it is a day for parties and celebrations in the middle of June. Every level of school will have an assembly where the pupils dress up and sing

Students celebrate the end of their *gymnasium* years with parties. The car takes them through town to show everyone they've finished. The caps, or *studentmösser*, show that they have graduated.

summer songs, such as 'The Time of Flowers is Coming' (Den Blomstertid nu kommer, Hymn 474 in the Swedish hymnal), hear talks from their teachers, and celebrate the beginning of summer and the end of another school year.

Students will not have to return until the second or third week in August. For those who are finishing secondary school, or *gymnasium*, at the age of 18 or 19, it is an even bigger celebration. They wear their white student caps with their best clothing all day, and take part in a special school assembly, often with prize-giving, student musicians, drama performances and art shows, and good luck talks from teachers and head teachers. As the assembly finishes, parents gather outside the school gates bearing flowers, champagne and large signs with baby photographs and the names of their grown-up children. The students often drive in groups around the town or city in open-top cars, shouting and laughing all the time, or have special family parties, or head off to balls and parties in the evening, or enjoy all three types of celebrations.

Midsummer's Day

This is, along with Christmas, one of the biggest holidays on the Swedish calendar, and one of the only ones which is particularly Swedish. It is celebrated on the Friday and Saturday of the week closest to 24 June, which is the real Midsummer's Day, and incorporates pagan summer solstice celebrations.

It is a holiday to be out in the country, and to celebrate the long days of summer. Even in the south of Sweden, there are more than 18 hours of daylight at this time of the year, and in the north, the sun does not really set at all. For children, the holiday begins in the afternoon, when the midsummer pole decorated with flowers and ribbons is raised. There are a few different theories about the midsummer pole, which is called a *majstång* or *midsommarstång* in Swedish. One is that it has always been raised at midsummer and that the *maj* in the name stems from an old Nordic word meaning 'decorated'. Another is that the tradition stems from the German maypole, which was raised on the first of May to

A traditional midsummer pole. The parents and children standing around are waiting for the singing and games around the midsummer pole to begin, wth music from the folk band.

celebrate the good weather. In most of Sweden, this is too early to celebrate good weather, so the tradition was moved to midsummer. Suffice it to say that it is now a definite symbol of midsummer.

When the midsummer pole is up, the children sing songs and dance traditional dances and games, pretending to be small frogs and other animals. As the afternoon turns into evening, it becomes time for the adults to celebrate. The menu for all is decided by tradition: new potatoes boiled with dill, several kinds of herring in sauces, beer and *snaps* to drink and strawberries with cream for afterwards. After the meal, the parties and dancing continue, often past sunrise the next day—but remember, sunrise can be as early as three o'clock in the morning!

Traditionally, unmarried girls would pick seven or nine different wild flowers and sleep with them under their pillows, in order to dream of the men they would marry. Midsummer is also a popular time for engagements and weddings.

Summer in Sweden

After midsummer, most Swedes have only a week left of work before Sweden shuts down for the summer holidays. Many factories and workplaces close for four weeks in July, and Swedes leave the cities and towns for small country houses on the sea and lakes. This is the time when they take the opportunity to enjoy the countryside and nature, during the warmest and lightest month of the year. Others travel abroad, to Mediterranean resorts and further afield. Summer camps and schools for children, as in the United States, are not common and most families holiday together.

Crayfish Parties: The End of Summer

In August the holidays are drawing to a close, the days are already getting shorter and cooler and children go back to school. But it is also time for crayfish (*kräftor*) parties and, soon after that, *surströmming* parties in the north of Sweden.

Crayfish parties began over a hundred years ago, when the crayfish season was limited in Sweden and people wanted

to celebrate being able to eat crayfish again. Traditionally, they should be held on the night of the first full moon after the beginning of the season, and they are jolly and informal parties, with piles of boiled crayfish, sauces to go with them, beer and *snaps*. The eating, drinking, reciting of crayfish rhymes and singing goes on until late at night. Crayfish are very messy to eat and you can buy paper bibs, napkins and even hats with pictures of crayfish on them, specially for these parties. The Swedish crayfish has nearly been fished out of existence, so most of the crayfish eaten at the parties are imported from Turkey, Spain or the US. You can buy frozen crayfish throughout the year but a crayfish party is a wonderful excuse to get together and eat and drink lots!

The *surströmming*, or fermented herring, parties are really only in the north of Sweden, but they are fascinating to the rest of Sweden. The fish is a very acquired taste, and takes a year to mature. In mid-August they are ready, and Swedes in the north get together to eat them with 'thin bread', small northern potatoes and lots of beer and *snaps*. Anyone who

The stuff that *surströmming* parties are made of: fermented herring, cheese, flatbread, potatoes and beer.

does not like *surstömming* will tell you that he or she needs to drink a lot to cope with the taste and smell.

A tradition in the south of Sweden is that of *ålagille*, or eel feasts. When the August moon begins to wane and the nights get darker, the eels cannot see the nets and are easily caught. These are eaten in many forms: fried, boiled, smoked and stuffed with different fillings. They are very rich with fat, and so the feasters wash them down with a few *snaps*.

All Saints Day

After the summer, Swedes settle back into work and school and get ready for the long winter. There are no more special holidays or celebrations until 1 November, All Saints Day, which is a solemn day for remembering the dead. It is always observed on the Saturday closest to 1 November. Halloween celebrations have become more popular in Sweden in the past ten years, but it is celebrated variously on the night before All Saints Day, on the 31 October, or any time around then. In addition, schoolchildren have a week's holiday around this time—they have already been studying for more than two months by now.

Saint Martin's Day

The tenth of November is Saint Martin's Day, a day celebrated not for the saint himself but for the geese which are eaten traditionally on this day. This particular tradition began in France, Saint Martin's homeland, centuries ago, and spread first to Germany and then to Sweden around the 1500s.

Saint Martin's Day is celebrated when the geese are the plumpest, and also when the year's wine is ready to be drunk (in France at least). In the southern province of Skåne, many Swedes go to restaurants to eat black soup (made traditionally with goose or pig blood, but now often with stock), roast goose and apple cake or *spettekaka*, a tall cake of egg yolks and sugar, baked on a spit. This is a meal Skåne-dwellers eat with pride but in fact it originated in a restaurant in Stockholm in the 1850s, influenced by the cooking of Renaissance France. Following Saint Martin's Day, there are only a few weeks until the first Sunday in Advent, and the country begins decorating and baking for Christmas again.

SWINGLISH OR SVENGELSKA?

CHAPTER 8

'Swedish has a far greater tolerance for ambiguous expressions than Greek. This is not always a bad thing. A vigorous 'We-ell' can be very useful in many situations. Over time, this characteristic of the Swedish language has also become a feature of Swedish culture. I know of no other country where the incomprehensible is cherished as warmly as in Sweden. It is the same with silence. We often see praise for a certain author, X, who has returned after 20 years of silence. As if not working were an achievement.'
—Theodor Kallifatides from *A New Land Outside My Window*, quoted in *The Swedish Book Review*, 2003.

DO YOU SPEAK ENGLISH?

Before you move to Sweden, everyone will tell you that all Swedes speak wonderful English. Then you move to Sweden and find out that the Swedes who have spoken English abroad speak wonderful English. The Swedes who haven't travelled abroad or have remained silent, don't. They have probably learned it in school (English language instruction has been compulsory for over 50 years) but that doesn't mean they are comfortable speaking it.

You can certainly get by in Sweden without learning the language, unlike many other countries, but you will miss a great deal by doing so. Swedish is not a difficult language for an English-speaker to learn, and speaking the language will greatly enhance your time in Sweden. If you hope to work or study in Sweden it is difficult to succeed in either without the language; but even if you just want to socialise with other Swedes, they will find it much easier and you will gain much more insight into the country, if you can converse in Swedish.

LEARNING SWEDISH

The words 'to teach' and 'to learn' are nearly the same thing in Swedish (*att lära* and *att lära sig*). One means 'to teach', and the other 'to teach oneself', which sums up the Swedish idea of guiding people through learning. If you have an opportunity to learn some Swedish before you come to Sweden, you will find it much easier to improve. Several companies, such as Linguaphone, produce book and tape combinations to teach yourself Swedish, or you can sometimes find Swedish lessons if you live near a big city.

LANGUAGE COURSES

However, if you come to Sweden knowing none of the language, you have a few further options. If you are registered and have a residence permit, you have the right to free Swedish language instruction through the SFI (Swedish for Immigrants) schools, although in some municipalities, students may have to pay a small fee towards their books and materials. These courses are arranged by the municipalities themselves and you should contact yours, once you have your personal number, to get a place. Depending on your location, your course may consist of regular daytime classes, a supported self-study programme, or distance learning via the Internet, and usually a combination of the three. In order to finish the programme, you will need to pass a national exam in Swedish at the end, called the *nationella prov*.

Course Structure

The SFI courses will take you through three stages: the first is basic Swedish, progressing onto more advanced grammar and then to more conversation. You take a test at the end of each level to ensure you can move onto the next one. At the end of the second level, you may take a test in basic Swedish history and customs. This is to help immigrants assimilate better into Swedish society. If you have not completed the equivalent of the nine years of compulsory schooling that Swedes have, you can also have basic classes and more Swedish lessons to bring you up to the same level.

Whilst enrolled in SFI classes, you may also be offered extra classes based around hobbies and conducted in Swedish. For example, sewing, guitar, baking or driving lessons are popular. You can practise Swedish in a relaxed environment and learn the specialised vocabulary you need.

Many SFI courses also offer practical job placements to help you with your Swedish. If you have the chance to do this, it may pay off in a permanent job offer in the future. It is worth remembering that your rights as an immigrant include the right to paid time off work for Swedish language instruction (through an SFI class). As far as your children are concerned, they have the right to extra Swedish language instruction through the schools to help get them to the same level as their classmates.

In addition, they have the right to 'mother tongue lessons' (lessons in their own language) to ensure that they have the best chance of being bilingual. These are intended to assist children who have another language at home. In practice, this is difficult to ensure if the child's native language is an unusual one, especially if you are living in a small town or rural area, but the authorities will do their best. The law stipulates that if five children in a municipality request the lessons (in the same language), they need to provide the teacher. In recent years, because of budget cuts, some native English-speakers have not been able to have extra lessons from *modersmålslärare*, or native tongue teachers, on the grounds that the children already study English as a foreign language in school and there is already a much greater overall exposure to English than to other immigrant languages. There is also a pilot project now working, to see if English can be taught at a younger age in schools and integrated with other subjects such as history or sciences.

If you do not want, or are not eligible, for SFI classes, there are also many evening classes and adult education classes in any number of subjects, including Swedish. Try the Swedish Folk University (Folkuniversitetet), or the union-run adult education organisations, such as ABF, TBV or Medborgarskolan. The cost is reasonable and you can choose whichever level and time suits you best.

A final option is either to employ a tutor or to try and pick it up as you go. Some companies will arrange language lessons for their employees and employees' families, as well. If you live with a Swede, try to practise it at home as much as possible—you'll be pleased by how much it helps you. There are also various websites which can help you with this; try typing 'swedish language lessons' into a search engine to find some.

Finding Fluency

There are said to be at least two stages of learning a foreign language before one is comfortable with it: the first is survival, enabling you to buy a train ticket or ask directions and the second is children's language, which means you will sound like a child grammatically and use a very limited vocabulary. Both of these stages are encouraging. It is when you get beyond these levels that you feel you have reached a plateau impossible to improve on. Your Swedish does not sound any better to you from week to week, and you can understand enough Swedish to hear all of your own mistakes and limitations. Push through this early fluency stage. Others will often hear your improvements, and even if you make lots of grammatical mistakes, they will often be able to understand you. Try to watch Swedish language television, listen to the radio or take out simplified Swedish books (called *lättlästa* or easy reading) from the library—they often have accompanying tapes as well.

THE SWEDISH LANGUAGE

Swedish is of the Indo-European language family, and has Germanic roots, as English does. Swedish speakers can usually understand some Norwegian and Danish, and vice versa. There are about 18 million speakers worldwide, with pockets of them in Finland and Estonia. If you can speak German, Dutch or Afrikaans in addition to English, you will find learning Swedish much easier. You may even be able to read some basic Swedish already. The same is not true for English speakers, but there are many words which will be familiar to English speakers, such as *man*, *fisk*, *hus* and *rum* which mean—you guessed it—'man', 'fish', 'house' and 'room'. Some words will also be familiar to people from the north of Britain—*barn* ('child') in Swedish is similar to the Scottish/North English word 'bairn' for a child. For German speakers, the connection is often closer; the Swedish *rådhus* ('town hall') sounds almost the same as the German *Rathaus*. Other words such as *billig* ('cheap' or 'inexpensive') are the same in both languages.

To make it easier still, Swedish, like English, has borrowed many words from foreign languages. A television is called a *TV* in Swedish, a pair of jeans is *ett par jeans* and so on. Some words are known in both English and the Swedish translation, such as 'software' (officially *mjukvara*, which is the literal translation of it, but the word *software* is at least as common). Many of these words start as unwelcome invaders until they are formally adopted by the Swedish Academy. One such recent adoption is the word 'live' when referring to music or a concert. Live music can now be referred to in Swedish as *live musik* and a live concert as *en live konsert*. If you aren't sure of the correct word in Swedish, it's often worth chancing an English or German word. Even if it's not correct, the Swede you are speaking with will often understand, and will appreciate you continuing in Swedish— with a one word exception.

Swedes are often said to sing while they speak. (Listen to Floyd, the Muppet's Swedish chef, singing 'Hurdy Gurdy' and you'll understand this.) If you can learn to sing a bit when you speak Swedish, you will be understood more easily as well. You may feel like you're mimicking Swedes in a way that might be rude, but in fact, you'll be imitating the way they speak their language, one of the best ways to learn a language yourself. English sounds very flat to most Swedes; try not to speak Swedish the same way.

BODY LANGUAGE

Non-verbal language is also important to learn. In general, Swedes do not gesticulate or move around very much when they are speaking, preferring to hold themselves still and rely on the words alone to convey their message. A popular non-word is the sound of people sucking in their breath sharply with a sound almost like 'hup'. This is difficult to describe but you will recognise it when you hear it. It has a multitude of meanings, from 'Okay, now we're finished eating, let's go' to 'What a sad story, what a shame' or perhaps, 'Nothing we can do about that I'm afraid' or 'I understand the problem now'. When you learn to inject this sound, with sharp breath intakes at the right places, you will really sound Swedish. There are many other non-word sounds in different accents and areas; you will get used to them as you learn the language. One thing you do need to remember though: throughout Sweden, they nod their heads to mean 'yes' and shake their heads to mean 'no'.

You don't really need to know any Swedish to understand this non-verbal international sign painted on the road. Even without much knowledge of the language, you will still be able to get by in Sweden. However, you will miss out on a lot of interaction with the Swedes.

Swedish Alphabet and Pronunciation

Swedish uses the Roman alphabet, but has 29 letters instead of 26. The last three are **å**, **ä** and **ö**.

- **å** is pronounced like *oa* in *boat*
- **ä** like *e* in *pet*
- **ö** like *i* in *bird*

Remember when you are looking a name up in the telephone book that these are the last three letters in the alphabet, so they won't be next to the ordinary 'A's or 'O's. Because the letters **v** and **w** are pronounced the same in Swedish, the telephone book will mix these up in the same section ('van' next to 'wan', for example).

Many of the letters, however, are pronounced very differently.

- **g** sounds like a *y* before the vowels **e**, **i**, **y**, **ä** and **ö** (called soft vowels)
- **j**, **dj**, **gj**, **hj** and **lj** also sound like a *y* before the soft vowels
- **k** sounds like a *ch* before the soft vowels
- **sch**, **sj**, **skj**, and **stj** are pronounced differently in the east and west. In the east, they have a strong *sh* sound. In the west, they sound a bit like the sound *hugh* in English, and it is not an easy sound to learn. Stick with the strong *sh* if you cannot do it and you will still be understood.
- **tj** sounds like *ch*

A further note about pronunciation: Swedish is one of the few tonal languages in Europe. This means that words which are pronounced nearly the same have different meanings, depending on the tone or emphasis you give to them. Don't worry about this in the beginning if you are not used to tonality in language; most of the words are so far apart in meaning that you will still be understood through context. As your Swedish vocabulary improves, you will need to learn the different stresses, because the words or phrases can also have similar meanings with varied nuances.

SWEDISH GRAMMAR

Swedish is one of the easiest languages, grammatically, for English speakers to learn. The main differences from English are that verbs do not need to agree with their subjects; there are two declensions of nouns; and the singular and plural forms of 'you' are different. Verbs, within the present or future or other tense, are the same regardless of what the subject (i.e. I, you, he, she, they, etc) is. Instead of having to remember 'I am', 'you are', 'he is', just remember the equivalent of 'I are', 'you are', 'he are' (in Swedish this is *jag är*, *du är* and *han är*).

The two declensions of nouns are common and neutral. Eighty percent of nouns are common, and the article for them is *en*. The rest are neutral and their article is *ett*. The definite article comes after the noun rather than before. This means that the word for 'girl', *flicka*, which is a common noun, becomes *en flicka* ('a girl') or *flickan* ('the girl') with an article. The same is true in the plural form (*flickor* is 'girls'; *flickorna*, 'the girls'). Whether a noun is *en* or *ett* must be learned by rote. Adjectives must also agree with the gender of the noun.

While English has one word for both the singular and plural forms of 'you', Swedish has two—*du* and *ni*. Ni can also be used to be polite to one person, but it is less common than using the equivalents in French or German. Most Swedes will say *du* to one another, even if they have never met before, and it has become the common usage in the past 40 years. Many say that *ni* is coming back into fashion, but this can offend the older generation so you may prefer to avoid it.

LEARNING DIFFICULTIES

Perhaps among the trickiest parts of learning the language are the different stresses and tonality. Help yourself through this by listening to as much Swedish as you can. If you don't know many Swedes, listen to the radio and television and hear the different ways they use their stresses. Swedes on the radio generally speak much clearer Swedish than in person which can be helpful.

Another difficulty, although you will appreciate it at first, is the prevalence of English as a second language. If you switch to English every time it gets difficult in Swedish it will take you longer to learn the language.

USEFUL PHRASES

To say 'yes' in Swedish, use *ja*, unless you are answering yes to a negative question, then you should use *jo*. For example, if someone asks you, "Don't you speak English?" and you answer *ja*, they will be confused—do you mean 'yes, I do speak English' or 'yes, I don't speak English'. Use *jo* to mean the first and *nej* to mean the second. Other 'yes' words include japp (sounds like the English 'yup') and javisst and jajamen which mean 'yes, of course' and 'yes, absolutely' respectively. Swedes will often make a noise which sounds like 'aw' to mean yes, or to confirm that they are listening and have understood.

To say hello, say *hej* (hay) which is equivalent to 'hello'. *Hej hej*, equally common, is like 'hi'. To be more formal, you can say *goddag*, *god morgon*, *god afton* or *god natt* which mean 'good day', 'good morning', 'good evening' and 'good

night' respectively. 'Goodbye' is generally *hej då* but can also be *adjö*, taken from the French word *adieu*. It's common to wish someone a good day or good time when leaving, by saying *ha det så bra*, or simply *ha det* ('have it so good', shortened to 'have it').

COURTESIES

'Thank you' is *tack* or sometimes *tackar* or *tack tack*. Swedes do not say the equivalent of 'thank you very much' as much as they say 'thank you', but if you want to be effusive, say *tack så mycket* ('thanks so much'). There is no Swedish word for 'please', so just use *tack* again when asking for something. Other options are *snälla* or *vänligen*, both of which mean variants on 'kind' or 'friendly'. The formal expression would be, 'Can you be kind and pass me the butter?' or else, 'Kind Maria, pass me the butter'. In Sweden it is more normal to leave out the 'please' equivalent and merely thank afterwards. Instead of 'you're welcome' or any other English equivalents, say *var så god*. This can also be an invitation for guests to help themselves or sit down. Its literal translation is 'be so good' and the unspoken end of the sentence is what you are being invited to do.

There is no word for 'sorry', so Swedes will use the equivalents of 'forgive me' (*förlåt mig*, shortened often to *förlåt*) or 'excuse me' (*ursäkta mig*, often shortened to *ursäkta*). If you want to ask if it's all right to do something, use the expressions, *Går det bra om...?* (literally, 'does it go well if...?') or *Gör det något om...?* ('does it matter if...?'). If you want to switch to English, ask if the person you are speaking with understands English by saying, *Pratar du engelska* or *Talar du engelska*. The Swedish language does not use as many capital letters as English or German, and while proper names and country names start with capital letters, language names and names of days and months do not. A final useful word is *hjälp* ('help') which sounds like 'yelp'—close enough to the English word in an emergency.

GREETINGS

Swedes generally shake hands and make eye contact when they greet people. If they have met before, they say *hej*. If they haven't, they often simply say their first name by way of introduction. It is more common for them to introduce themselves than for their host to formally introduce them. Some Swedes have adopted the European greeting of a single kiss and/or a hug, but it is not very common.

Personal space is important to Swedes, and it is not often they will strike up a conversation with a stranger in a train or other public place. If you try it may be welcomed but it may also be seen as threatening. Silence between friends is seen as companionable and not at all worrying. When Swedes do talk amongst friends, they do not often interrupt each other and are not comfortable with interruptions. They tend to speak less overall, and more directly. They rarely gush and like to tell it as it is. Exaggerated expressions common in English (such as 'I love ice-cream' or 'losing that umbrella was tragic') are not often heard in Swedish.

TELEPHONE SWEDISH

Swedes answer the telephone with their names or their telephone numbers, rather than 'hello'. Sometimes this is the whole name, sometimes just the surname. If you telephone and want to speak to someone you should ask, *Kan jag få prata med...?* ('Can I get to speak with...?') Two answers you may encounter are *Kan du dröja?* or *Ett ögonblick* ('Can you wait?' or 'Just a minute'). Swedes do not appreciate abruptness on the telephone, and you should always say goodbye before hanging up.

DAYS, DATES, TIME AND NUMBERS

Dates are written backwards for an English-speaker. Christmas Day in 1996 is therefore written as '961225' officially. You may also see it written as '25/12 1996' informally. Time runs on a twenty-four hour clock, so there is no am or pm.

To ask the time, say *Vad är klockan?* ('What's the clock?') Half past the hour means half way to the next one, so the Swedish *halv tre* ('half three') is really 2:30 in English. It is not uncommon to use the twenty-four hour clock in everyday speech, so that while it is usual to agree to meet at *halv tre*, don't be surprised if someone suggests meeting at 14:30 instead. The abbreviation for the time is *kl*. (For example, the train leaves at *kl* 18:00.)

The days of the weeks and the months are very similar to the English words. The week begins on Monday and ends on Sunday, with the Swedish words as follows:

- *måndag*   Monday
- *tisdag*   Tuesday
- *onsdag*   Wednesday
- *torsdag*   Thursday
- *fredag*   Friday
- *lördag*   Saturday
- *söndag*   Sunday

The months, which, like the days, do not start with a capital letter are:

- *januari*   January
- *februari*   Feburary
- *mars*   March
- *april*   April
- *maj*   May
- *juni*   June
- *juli*   July
- *augusti*   August
- *september*   September
- *oktober*   October
- *november*   November
- *december*   December

However, unlike in English, these are not usually abbreviated to jan, feb, etc.

When Swedes write numbers, they switch the commas and decimal points that an English-speaker would normally use. Therefore six thousand Swedish crowns is written 'SEK6.000', and five and a half percent is written '5,5%'.

USEFUL ABBREVIATIONS

f Kr	*före Kristi*	BC
e Kr	*efter Kristi*	AD
t ex	*till exempel*	for example; e.g.
osv	*och så vidare*	and so on, etc.
t o m	*till och med*	until and including
fr o m	*från och med*	from and including
bl a	*bland annat*	among others
ca		circa
dvs	*det vill säga*	that is to say; i.e.
f d	*före detta*	previously
f n	*för närvarande*	presently
p g a	*på grund av*	on account of
s k	*så kallad*	so called

All of these abbreviations are commonly written as such, even in the middle of literary works or newspapers. However, in spoken Swedish, the full expression is used. The United Nations is 'the FN', the European Union 'the EU', the Olympic Games 'OS' and World Championships are called 'VM', and all of these abbreviations are used commonly in spoken as well as written Swedish.

ENGLISH IN SWEDEN

If you are tired of speaking Swedish, or are only going to be in the country for a short time and don't want to learn the language, in spite of my exhortations to do so, you'll be pleased to know that you can certainly function without the language. As mentioned, English has been a compulsory subject in Swedish schools for over 50 years and many Swedes do like to practise their English. You will often find that workers in cafés, banks and shops are very helpful even if their English is a bit rusty. The younger generation speaks generally excellent English, and many companies use English as their official language.

ACCOMMODATING FOREIGN LANGUAGES

One of your rights as an immigrant is to an interpreter when dealing with the authorities. If you need to have an immigration interview, it can be conducted in English if necessary. You can also take your driving licence test in English, find an English-speaking doctor or health clinic and, in the larger cities, send your children to English-speaking schools and attend English-speaking religious services.

Swedish libraries provide books and tapes in many foreign languages. In any bookshop, there is likely to be a selection of English-language books, and many academic books or less popular works are only available in English (the Swedish book-buying market is not large enough to make translations viable for these books). You will usually be able to find British newspapers on sale on the same day in the larger cities and a few days later elsewhere, while North American, Australasian and other newspapers are available in the larger cities a few days after publication. Many specialist magazines do not have equivalents in Swedish and so are on sale in English, or can be ordered by a good newsagent. The government also sponsors a small weekly newspaper of Swedish immigrant news, which is available in all of the main immigrant languages (including English) as well as in simplified Swedish.

RADIO AND TELEVISION

Many of the programmes on Swedish television are bought from overseas, and subtitled rather than dubbed, so you will be able to follow many of the shows familiar to you. Films and videos are also subtitled rather than dubbed, and the newest Hollywood releases are often screened earlier in Sweden than in Britain. Note, however, that children's programmes and films are usually dubbed.

Apart from Swedish television, foreign channels such as BBC Prime, Sky, CNN, Eurosport and MTV Europe, as well as various French, German, Danish and Norwegian channels (depending on where you live) are also available if you have a cable connection; most apartment blocks do.

Swedish radio offers specific programming in immigrant languages as well. If you buy a good shortwave radio you will be able to access BBC World Service, Voice of America and various other overseas programmes. Some of the local Swedish stations broadcast news or other programmes in English occasionally—look out for them in the programme schedules of the newspaper.

IMMIGRANT GROUPS

If you need to speak to someone in your own language, join one of the many immigrant groups which offer help, support, companionship, friendship, volunteer work or a combination of all five. Many long term foreign residents still attend these groups to celebrate national holidays and to keep in touch with their countries. They range from being well organised—with bylaws, statutes and formal connections with the embassy (like the American Women's Club)—to just an informal group of countrymen who meet occasionally for gossip and to catch up. You can find out about them through the phone book, other local foreigners or your embassy. For native English speakers, going online to some of the expatriate websites is a good way to meet people. Try the following:

- http://www.amerikanska.com
- http://www.lostinsweden.com
- http://www.mumsinsweden.com (for those of you with children)

With such a good backup system, you might feel even more inspired to learn Swedish. Although you can manage without it, you will get much more out of the country and enjoy it much more as soon as you learn. In fact, the single best piece of advice anyone moving to Sweden can get is to learn at least some of the language, either before you arrive or soon afterwards. Any of the negative things about moving to a foreign country in general, and a cold, northern country like Sweden in particular, will seem minor compared with the positive aspects of learning about a new country when you can understand what is going on.

Sweden's beautiful natural scenery makes outdoor camping a popular activity among the locals.

Kalmar Castle was built as a defence tower in the 12th century. This was where the Kalmar Union was formed in 1397, and today the castle is considered one of Sweden's most beautiful buildings.

The Scandinavian Mountains run in between Norway and Sweden, offering visitors spectacular sights along the nature walk.

A bonfire burns brightly as Swedes gather around and sing. According to tradition, bonfires help to scare away witches and evil spirits that are visiting the devil.

In Sweden, many cottages and houses are painted in Falu Red, a traditional Swedish colour that originated from a copper mine at Falun.

BUSINESS IN SWEDEN

CHAPTER 9

'He had nothing to promise her, therefore he kept still;
a spoken word and a promise carried weight;
one had to answer for it, it could never be taken back.'
—Karl Oskar in Vilhelm Moberg's *The Emigrants*

ECONOMY AND INDUSTRY

Sweden has grown, in under a hundred years, from a poor agrarian society to a high-tech and modern industrial and service economy. The traditional exports of Sweden were timber and iron, and both still play a part in the economy today, with engineering products, car and aircraft manufacture and the paper industry all having grown from the forestry and metals industries. Since the global downturn in 2008, the economy has contracted sharply and it remains to be seen how important industry, including the automotive industry, will remain in the Swedish economy.

Major Industries

Among the largest industries in Sweden are the engineering and automotive industries. Both Volvo and Saab-Scania are important employers in Sweden, as are Ericsson, ABB, Electrolux and SKF in engineering and manufacturing. Much of the success of these companies is due to strong export performances—the Swedish market is too small to support a large company on its own. Because of this, the US economic situation in 2008 has affected both Saab and Volvo Car greatly and their future is uncertain.

The forestry industry provides jobs for many in the north and, indirectly, for many in the pulp and paper industries in the whole of Sweden. The paper industry alone accounts for 11 per cent of Sweden's total industrial value. Firms such as Stora, SCA, Tetra-Pak and Mölnlycke work with forest products.

The assembly line at Volvo's Torslanda plant. Volvo is one of the two automotive giants in Sweden who contribute greatly to Sweden's economy.

Other natural resources, the metals and iron ore in Sweden, have provided work for miners in northern Sweden for years. The mining industry is in decline, but the Swedish steel industry, after much modernisation and investment, is still successful, exporting 80 per cent of its products.

Other important industries are the telecommunications and computer industry, the pharmaceutical industry (with AstraZenecca and Pharmacia as the largest companies) and the arms industry (with both Bofors and such aeronautical companies as Saab as big players). Many Swedes have now found work in service industries, as the economic downturn of the late 1990s hit Sweden and the many Swedes who worked in telecommunications and the IT industries hard. The service industry has continued to grow in importance and remains one of the stronger employers in Sweden.

WORKING CONDITIONS

The historic importance of labour unions in Sweden has meant that Swedish employees have excellent working conditions compared with most countries. The majority of Swedes belong to one of the large unions, such as the LO (170,000 members), with mostly blue-collar workers; the TCO, with mostly white-collar workers; or the SACO/SR, the union for academics. There is also a union for employers, called the Swedish Employers' Confederation (SAF), with over 55,000 member companies.

The unions have worked together for such labour legislation as the Security of Employment Act (1974), the Act on Equality Between Men and Women (1980) and the Co-determination Act (1977) which ensures employee participation in decision making. The first Act ensures that no employee can be dismissed or demoted unless there is an objective reason for doing so, and that no employee's job description can be changed without consultation with the employee's union. This has meant an increase in job security in general for Swedes, although this has been tested in the recent recession. Other union victories over the past hundred years have resulted in reduced working hours, increased holiday time, the right to leaves of absence for studying or for having a child, and better pay settlements.

WORKING HOURS AND LEISURE TIME

Working hours for most Swedes are between 8:00 am or 9:00 am and 4:00 pm or 5:00 pm. Most work between 40 hours a week full time—and overtime is regulated by the Working Hours Act—to a maximum amount in a month and a year. Workers are entitled to a meal break after five hours of work, and must be allowed at least 36 hours of leisure time in every week, usually at the weekends. A large percentage of working mothers work part time; and any parent's right to work only 75 per cent of full time is protected until their child is eight years old (older in special cases).

By law, an employee is entitled to 25 days of paid holiday a year, and there are also 12 public holidays. When a public holiday falls on a Thursday or a Tuesday, the Friday or the Monday are called 'squeeze-days' (*klämdager*) and many employees work a little extra every day in order to take these days off. These are given in lieu of overtime in many companies. Many Swedes choose to take three or four weeks of their holiday in July, and a company is required to allow four continuous weeks of holiday between June and August, unless there is a collective agreement stating otherwise. Sweden comes close to closing down during July but since joining the European Union, more companies are working at least partially throughout the summer.

More labour legislation ensures that if you are too ill to work, your employer is required to pay part of your salary on the second to the 13th day of your illness. The first day of illness, called a *karensdag*, is unpaid to discourage workers ringing in sick for extra time off. After the 13th day, the state takes over and pays your sickness benefit. If your child is ill, you are entitled to time off to take care of him or her. Parental leave on the birth of a child is granted equally to mothers and fathers, who can share up to 390 days leave of absence at 80 per cent of pay, with a further 90 days at a fixed rate. Sixty of these days cannot be signed over to the other parent; otherwise the parents can divide the leave as they choose.

Employment Contracts

Contracts are legally binding in Sweden, whether written or verbal, and you should receive written notification of your terms and conditions of employment within a month of starting work. You are protected against unfair dismissal,

Many Swedes work in modern office blocks, like the one to the left in this picture. In the centre, Göteborg's opera house continues to revitalise a harbour front which has, in the past, suffered from a decline in the shipping industries.

and have certain entitlements in any permanent job. The exception is if your contract stipulates that it is a temporary contract, with fewer rights, and of course, during your initial probationary period. Pay is either as a salary—paid weekly or monthly—or as a wage, paid depending on how many hours you have worked in a given period. There should be a health and safety representative at every firm employing more than five people, and employees are insured by law against work injury.

SWEDES AND WORK

Traditionally, most Swedes were employed by large employers (the public sector or one of the major companies) with the job security and career development that it implies. Self-employed workers tended to be in specific sectors, such as retail. Since the economic downturn and IT boom of the 1990s, as well as the uncertainty following the 2008 financial upheaval, however, the face of Swedish work life has changed. Workers no longer expect a job for life, and short-term contracts are all the more common than before. Temporary agencies are now allowed and an increasing number of people have set themselves up as self-employed workers in more and more sectors. Sweden is now considered to be a fertile ground for start-up companies, thanks to the highly educated workforce, the low corporate tax (compared with other European countries) and the advanced technological culture. It remains to be seen how this shift will change the way Swedes actually are at work.

SWEDES AT WORK

Swedes have a strong work ethic, but guard their private time fiercely. This doesn't mean they will never work overtime, just that they will need to be convinced there is a good reason for it. Their family life is very important to them, and given the Swedish propensity for signing up for sports and cultural clubs, lessons and activities, combined with dual-career couples, their free time will often be fully scheduled, and they will not want to rearrange it at short notice. This is not to say they won't do so, if they're convinced it's necessary. When you work with Swedish colleagues you should respect the work hours they keep. They will be punctual in both arriving and leaving and that, a Swede will tell you, is how it should be. By the same token, business entertaining will generally not be in private homes, although it is more common for Swedes to take work home now than before.

Swedish business structures generally tend to be flat, rather than hierarchical, as in the pyramid structures of many American and British firms. Of course the managing director is the boss, but he or she will usually be accessible to all employees, and relations between different job levels are often open and informal. The workplace itself will often feel quite informal, with casual dress and décor common. Part of the conformity and culture in Sweden means that nobody wants to make it seem like they feel they're better than anyone else. Therefore nobody will want to show off with top of the range business clothes. A top level briefcase doesn't spell status in Sweden. Rather it makes your colleagues wonder 'who does he think he is?'. Suits and formal attire are common in some industries, but not necessary in the majority, and jeans are not unusual even among doctors and bank managers. Smart casual probably defines the dress code of most offices, although as conformists Swedes do like to follow fashion, it will be reasonably new smart casual.

Swedes like to feel comfortable and happy at work, and many firms have sports clubs and special interest groups who meet at lunchtime or after work. It's not unusual for workers to take a company-sponsored long weekend skiing in the mountains, or in another city, as a team building exercise. Offices are often comfortably furnished, again with fewer hierarchical differences between personal workspaces.

As with Swedes at school and at play, consensus is important in business life. It's better to reach a solution through co-operation, even if it takes longer, than through an independent decision handed down. In some instances, a decision can take two or three times longer because nobody wants to overrule the dissenters. Swedes learn in preschool that *alla ska vara med* ('everyone must be included'), and it is a lesson they take to heart. In keeping with their national

Office buildings in Stockholm.

character, Swedish employees downplay their achievements and don't look for extra credit for work well done. The qualities which characterise the Swedes in other areas, such as caution, pragmatism, efficiency and quietness, are all evident in the way a Swede conducts business.

One of the important things to remember when you are working with Swedes, therefore, is to aim to work in a team, and not for individual credit. Swedes praise less and there is more of an attitude of 'of course I have done that well because it is my job'. You can expect less praise in general from a Swedish manager, but it does not mean he or she is not equally happy with your work.

In addition, Swedes prefer to be cautious about what is achievable as well. Whereas an American may promise 'we'll deliver next month' knowing that it is 90 per cent possible, a Swede will only allow that it is possible. Swedes never want to be in the position of apologising for not doing something they have said they will do. For this reason, you can be sure they will deliver if they say they will. If they tell you something may take two months, because they are overloaded right now, you may have it delivered within one, and wonder why they couldn't have been more optimistic. The answer: because they would not want to have to go back on their word. You should also underpromise when doing business with Swedes.

FINDING WORK AS AN IMMIGRANT

In recent years, the unemployment rate has been high for Swedes and immigrant unemployment has been higher still. If you can build on any Swedish contacts in your field before you move, you will improve your chances of finding work. Contacts in any job search are crucial but in Sweden, many jobs are never advertised at all and according to one study, 50 per cent of workers find their jobs via contacts. These need not be professional contacts; your father-in-law's tennis partner may know of an opening and that may be all you need. This is why work placements are so valuable especially for immigrants. The wider a contact network you can build up the easier it will be to find work.

Otherwise, if you have not been transferred by your home company to Sweden, your job search may start at the Arbetsförmedlingen (Employment Office). Any immigrant who is attending SFI language classes can also ask the SFI consultant for help with the Arbetsförmedlingen system. Each Employment Office has several consultants, who will interview you to try to place you in the right job. In cities, the Employment Offices may handle only one type of industry, so you should check that you are in the right place for what you want to do.

Once you have completed the forms and your interview, you can receive help with applying for jobs and for training and courses. If you are entitled to unemployment benefit, you may be required to attend the Employment Office to collect it, or to log into to their website to look for jobs a certain number of times. Job vacancies are advertised on the Employment Office's website at http://www.ams.se. After a certain period of unemployment you may be entitled to job-hunting classes, covering interview skills, letter-writing skills, and learning how to target yourself. Your consultant can help you find out about these options.

In addition, there are now many recruitment, placement and search firms, the majority of which have got websites where you can register your details and apply for advertised jobs. You can find links to major ones from the Employment Office's website. Many employers place advertisements in the local or national newspapers, although this is not as common as in the UK or US. Check the small adverts if you are interested in casual work, as many private employers advertise there. If you want to target a certain type of company, a speculative letter to companies found in the yellow pages of the telephone directory, followed up by a telephone call, can work well. You don't necessarily need to write the initial letter in Swedish, especially if it is not very good and you want to highlight your English skills, but it will be difficult to get a job without any conversational Swedish. In general, the etiquette is that if a job is advertised in Swedish, you should write your application in Swedish; if the job advert is in English, you should write your application in English.

If you are under 25, you should look into special practical places, where the government pays you a salary while you gain experience in working for a firm. The firms often take on the 'practice workers' as permanent employees at the end of the six-month placement.

Qualifications and Language

One of the challenges of finding work in Sweden, aside from casual work, is that many professions require Swedish qualifications and so you may have to retrain. Most jobs in Sweden require specific qualifications, and while in other countries, a general university degree will open doors to many careers, in Sweden you are expected to have specific training. Currently there are 32 regulated professions in Sweden which require specific training, such as lawyers, doctors, teachers and accountants. Should you already have such specialist training from your home country then you can have your qualifications assessed by the appropriate agency. There is a list of the appropriate agencies on the website for the Swedish National Agency for Higher Education (Högskoleverket, http:// www.hogskoleverket.se). Even if you have a general university degree, it may be worthwhile to have your education evaluated and translated into the Swedish system; again contact the Swedish National Agency for Higher Education for the forms and information.

Another difficulty is that you will need excellent Swedish in many jobs, and your proficiency in English will not always be a significant advantage to an employer who may have many Swedish employees with an excellent command of English. Many companies do use English as their company language, but the actual day-to-day meetings and water cooler conversations will be in Swedish. For this reason, be wary of assurances that it will be easy for you, as an English speaker, to find work in Sweden. It is not easy for anyone, including Swedes. Part of this is because of current unemployment rates, which are forecast to soar in 2010, but part of this is because it is expensive to hire people in Sweden due to high social contributions, and it is even more expensive to fire people. Swedes are, at any rate, naturally cautious and staff turnover tends to therefore be low in Swedish companies.

Good Possibilities for Work

Many immigrants work as foreign language teachers in private and adult education schools (to work in the Swedish school system, you will need a full teaching qualification from Sweden or another European Union country), in restaurants and pubs, and in casual jobs at least initially. There are often English language teaching opportunities, through both business English centres and evening classes, but there are a lot of well established teachers with whom new arrivals will have to compete. Once you start getting work, you will gradually be able to build up your hours, especially if the school realises that you are settling in Sweden. The better qualified you are (either with a TEFL certificate or in business in your home country), the better the pay and conditions you will get, so it's worth thinking about getting some experience before moving to Sweden.

Looking for restaurant work is often best done in person. Turn up at the place you want to work and see if they need help. Around Easter is an excellent time to start looking in many areas, because many restaurants have outdoor serving areas open only in the summer months, and need to hire extra staff for the summer. There are many English-style pubs and restaurants, some of which are owned by expatriate Brits, Irish, Australians or Americans. The language spoken at work is sometimes English and it's a good idea to target these places first.

STARTING YOUR OWN BUSINESS

If casual work or teaching aren't suitable, and assuming that your Swedish linguistic skills aren't up to the mark for you to find a job, you may wish to look into starting your own business. Because of the difficulty of getting jobs without contacts or Swedish qualifications, a large number of immigrants do this, importing goods from their own countries, running shops or cafés, working as business consultants or offering services such as translation.

Many evening class centres offer courses on starting your own business (called *Starta eget*—'start your own'), and they can offer a lot of useful advice. Some of these courses are in English, although most are in Swedish. If you are interested in starting an import-export business, you may like to ask the Swedish Trade Council (at http://www.swedishtrade.com) for advice. They can provide useful information about customs, importing regulations and trade links with foreign firms.

Information for New Business Owners

- All new companies in Sweden must register with the Register of Companies, the tax office and the social security office.
- Employees' rights are strictly regulated and you should make certain that you are up-to-date with these before employing extra staff. SAF, the trade union for employers, can help you with information about this, as can the Confederation of Swedish Enterprise at:

    http://www.svensktnaringsliv.se

    or the Invest in Sweden Agency at:

    http://www.isa.se.
- You can usually raise finance, even for a foreign company, through a Swedish bank.
- You may be eligible for grants or assistance to help you start a business and the Employment Office should be able to advise you on this, or one of the entrepreneurship organisations such as Nutek. You can also get information from the local authorities (*länsstyrelsen*) or your local tax office, who run courses for self-employed people.

VOLUNTEER WORK

The whole concept of volunteer work in Sweden is different from that in the UK, US or other countries, but it is slowly changing. Since the welfare state was introduced, most Swedes felt that volunteer work, like charity, ought not to be needed. Many Swedes volunteered countless hours for sports groups, art groups or political parties, but the idea of volunteering to run a soup kitchen or to work in inner city literacy programmes was not only unheard of, but considered unnecessary. If people couldn't read then it was the government's responsibility to amend that, and then it should be trained paid teachers helping them, not good-natured literate volunteers.

As Sweden moves on, though, it is becoming apparent that the welfare state cannot provide everything. More and more people are agreeing to volunteer for such groups as the Red Cross, in the same way as they have always raised money for their children's sports groups, and helped publicise amateur art exhibitions. The idea of a bake sale to raise money for a school may still be hard for Swedes to swallow, however. To find out more about opportunities, contact your local volunteer bureau (http://www.volontarbyran.org/).

SWEDEN AT A GLANCE

CHAPTER 10

'Now, what I want is Facts ...
Facts alone are wanted in life.'
—Mr Gradgrind in *Hard Times* by Charles Dickens

Official Name
Sweden

Capital
Stockholm

Flag
Blue with a golden yellow cross extending to the edges of the flag; the vertical part of the cross is shifted to the hoist side in the style of the Dannebrog (Danish flag).

National Anthem
Sång till Norden (Song of the North)

Time
Greenwich Mean Time plus 1 hour (GMT + 0100). Daylight savings, from the last Sunday in March until the last Sunday in October every year, is GMT plus 2 hours, and co-ordinated with the European Union. Swedes commonly use the 24-hour clock when referring to the time.

Telephone Country Code
46

Land
Located in Northern Europe, bordering the Baltic Sea, Gulf of Bothnia, Kattegat and Skagerrak, between Finland and Norway

Area
total: 449,964 sq km (279,595 sq miles)
land: 410,934 sq km (255,343 sq miles)
water: 39,030 sq km (24,252 sq miles)

Highest Point
Kebnekaise (2,111 m / 6,925 ft)

Climate
Temperate in the south with cold, cloudy winters and cool, partly cloudy summers; subarctic in the north

Natural Resources
Iron ore, copper, lead, zinc, gold, silver, tungsten, uranium, arsenic, feldspar, timber, hydropower

Population
9,263,872 (February 2009)

Ethnic Groups
Indigenous population: Swedes plus Finnish and Sami minorities; foreign-born or first-generation immigrants: Finns, Yugoslavs, Danes, Norwegians, Greeks, Turks

Religion
Lutherans make up 87 per cent; the remaining 13 per cent are Roman Catholics, Orthodox Christians, Baptists, Muslims, Jews or Buddhists

Official Languages
Swedish, small Sami- and Finnish-speaking minorities

Government Structure
Constitutional monarchy

Administrative Divisions

21 counties (known as *län*, in the singular or plural form): Blekinge, Dalarnas, Gävleborgs, Gotlands, Hallands, Jämtlands, Jönköpings, Kalmar, Kronobergs, Norrbottens, Örebro, Östergötlands, Skåne, Södermanlands, Stockholms, Uppsala, Värmlands, Västerbottens, Västernorrlands, Västmanlands, Västra Götalands

Currency

Swedish krona (SEK)

Gross Domestic Product (GDP)

US$348.6 billion (2008 est.)

Agricultural Products

Barley, wheat, sugar beets, meat, milk

Industries

Iron and steel, precision equipment (bearings, radio and telephone parts, armaments), wood pulp and paper products, processed foods, motor vehicles

Exports

Machinery, motor vehicles, paper products, pulp and wood, iron and steel products, chemicals

Imports

Machinery, petroleum and petroleum products, chemicals, motor vehicles, iron and steel; foodstuffs, clothing

Measurements

All measurements are in the metric system, including temperature (Celsius), weights (kilograms and grams), liquids (litres) and distances (kilometres and metres). There is also an old Nordic measurement still in common use: the Swedish mile (en mil), which equals ten km. For this reason, if you talk about the English or American mile, you should call it the English mile to differentiate.

Airports
254. Stockholm's main airport is Arlanda; Göteborg's main airport is Landvetter and Malmö's is Sturup. In addition, there are smaller airports serving the main and smaller cities.

FAMOUS PEOPLE
Statesmen
- Dag Hammarskjöld, Director-General of the United Nations
- Olof Palme, prime minister assassinated in 1981
- Raoul Wallenberg, saviour of thousands of Jews during World War II
- Hans Blix, head of the UN weapons inspectors

Arts, Literature and Science
- Astrid Lindgren, children's author
- August Strindberg, playwright
- Ingmar Bergman, film director
- Anders Zorn, painter
- Greta Garbo, actress
- Carl von Linné, botanist and scientist
- ABBA, 1970s popgroup

Industrialists/Business
- Alfred Nobel, inventor of dynamite and founder of the Nobel Prizes
- Ingvar Kamprad, founder of IKEA

Sports
- Björn Borg, tennis player
- Annika Sörenstam, golfer
- Ingmar Stenmark, skiier
- Carolina Kluft, heptathlete

Places of Interest
- Stockholm, for the 'Venice of the north', the capital city on the water
- The university cities of Uppsala and Lund

Stockholm, the capital of Sweden, is also the largest city in the country. The city is actually made up of 14 islands, all connected by bridges. The city centre is right in the middle and virtually sits on water.

Limestone formations off the coast of Gotland island.

- The island of Gotland, with the Hanseatic town of Visby
- The west coast, in particular the rocky coasts of Bohuslän, with the island town of Marstrand, as well as the second city of Göteborg
- The steamboat journey along the Göta Canal from Göteborg to Stockholm

This leaves out thousands of places in the beautiful forests, along the beaches of the coasts, and in the mountains of the north. There is much to discover.

CULTURE QUIZ

Now that you have some inside knowledge of the way Swedish society operates, you can test yourself with the following questions. As with any culture, there are not always definitive responses to every situation but the Swedish character is such that in most cases, the best response should be fairly obvious to you.

After the initial settling-in period and as you begin to feel as though you fit into your new surroundings, the benefits and drawbacks of living and staying in Sweden will become a part of your own lifestyle. When you have reached this point, congratulations—now you are a real Svensson!

SITUATION 1
You have been invited to a Swedish colleague's home for dinner at 7:30 pm. You are looking forward to seeing their home and eating Swedish food, and have brought some wine to take with you. They live on the other side of town and there are only two buses an hour to their area. One would get you there at 7:45 pm and the other at 7:15 pm. Do you:

Ⓐ Decide you'll drive; you don't plan to get drunk anyway.
Ⓑ Take the latter; there's nothing worse than being early to someone's house, and you've always heard that 20 minutes late is simply fashionable.
Ⓒ Take the earlier bus, even though it's a nuisance.

Comments
You could drive, but then you won't be able to drink at all. It's not a question of not getting drunk in Sweden. The drink driving laws are so strict that you'll need to refuse the wine you're taking with you. However, if you do drive, your hosts will certainly understand and respect that you cannot drink that evening.

Taking the late bus is the only 'wrong' option—it will mean that you arrive later than the stated 7:30 pm time. This is the time that your host and hostess are expecting you to arrive at their house, and they will have timed their cooking of the meal and the rest of the evening accordingly. Punctuality is expected and arriving late is generally considered impolite.

If other guests are involved and you are late, they will all be waiting for you, probably uncomfortably. A cocktail hour is not common in Sweden. The best option is to take the early bus and you can arrive at their door at 7:30 pm exactly. If you're five or ten minutes early, that's fine; Swedes will be used to it.

SITUATION 2

You and your child are taking the bus, or the tram or subway. He is complaining and wants some chocolate from one of the kiosks, but you don't want him to spoil his dinner. He starts to work himself up into a state and screams and, in the crowded area, you are not sure what to do. Do you:

A Start to scream back at him to stop him.

B Give him a sharp slap and tell him he'll be in trouble when you get home.

C Ask him calmly (through gritted teeth, if necessary) not to scream. If necessary, get off the bus until he stops, or to cuddle him.

D Warn him he'll be punished by his other parent when you are get home.

Comments

Every culture has different ways of raising children and just because you have moved to Sweden does not mean you need to adopt all of their ideas about children. However, you should be aware that option **B** is illegal wherever you are in Sweden, and therefore cannot be recommended.

You may not threaten or physically harm a child in public or at home. If you try to intimidate your child with promises of punishment at home, you will probably violate this law as well. Swedes prefer not to intervene in family matters but if they think you are harming your child, they may well.

Screaming back will also incur the disapproval of all around you (not least because of the increased noise).

Swedes are not above admonishing you if they disapprove. The Swedish option would be **C**—frustrating at times, but moderate.

SITUATION 3

You are working in a company that needs an overhaul of its ordering system. Part of your job is to work out which system would be most effective. You settle down to work on this and, at around 4:00 pm one afternoon, you come up with a solution. It's such a good solution that you feel it needs to be implemented immediately. Do you:

A Call an immediate meeting of all staff and explain the new system to them.

B Send a memorandum around to everyone, telling them about the new system.

C Send a memorandum around to everyone, asking them to come to a meeting the next day to talk about ways of implementing the new system, should everyone agree it is the best way forward.

Comments

Option **B** is the most efficient, which would seem Swedish, but in fact it would come across as impersonal, and worse, imperious. The idea of consensus is very important to Swedes, in business as well as everyday life and your colleagues will expect to be involved in the decision. (This is becoming more and more true in everyday business life in many other countries also.)

The same lack of consultation is a problem with Option **A**, but a bigger problem is going to be that many people in Sweden work from 8:00 am–4:00 pm, and they will not want to stay back for an unplanned meeting. Swedish workers are industrious and won't, in general, refuse to work overtime but they value their free time and won't want to work over if it isn't absolutely necessary.

Option **C** is the best, but make sure that when you present your solution at the meeting you are ready for a discussion of the system before it is adopted through consensus.

SITUATION 4

You are at a party where you know only a few of the guests. Most of the others seem to know each other and you feel uneasy as you cannot keep up with their Swedish. Do you:

A Wait for your host to introduce you to some of the other guests.

B Go up to the other guests and introduce yourself, asking in English what their name is and what they do.

C Turn to another guest and try to start a conversation in Swedish, asking also if they speak English.

D Find your host and ask if he will introduce you to some guests who speak English. You think, although you don't say this, that introducing you to people you can speak with is one of his duties as host.

Comments

Swedes prefer to introduce themselves, usually through shaking your hand and saying their names at the same time. You should say your name back while still shaking their hand. When you arrive, introduce yourself to the guests already there, rather than them making the effort to introduce themselves to you (another reason to arrive early at a party). Therefore options **A** and **D** are not the best ones.

Option **B** is good, but don't ask new acquaintances what they do at a party. Business and pleasure are kept separate and it is not common to identify yourself through your work to the same extent as it is in other countries. Having to speak English may make some Swedes nervous or uncomfortable, so you may have to try this option with several different people.

Option **C** is probably the best one. Many people approached this way will switch to English after you have tried in Swedish. If you introduce yourself before starting the conversation, you will fit in best.

SITUATION 5

You are taking your child to her new preschool. She will be at preschool every day while you work or study, and you are worried about her being happy there. When you arrive, you see some of the children playing out in the snow. You go into the centre and are met by one of the childcare workers who explains that everybody else is out on a long walk in the woods. You are a little surprised by both of these things. Do you:

Ⓐ Say how wonderful that the children get so much outdoor playing time; it's so healthy for them.

Ⓑ Ask how long the children will be playing outside, and if they go outside even when it is actually snowing, and if your child can stay inside on such days as she's not used to such cold weather. Explain your child is not used to long walks and would get too tired and upset by it.

Ⓒ Wonder why no one is playing inside where there are such nice toys.

Ⓓ Ask if they have an educational schedule you can see.

Comments

Any of these options are completely normal for a non-Swede to ask, but option **Ⓐ** is the truly Swedish choice. Swedes are very keen on children having unstructured play time and on being outside for fresh air. Therefore it would be unusual for any of them to ask why no one is playing indoors (option **Ⓒ**). Similarly, option **Ⓑ** would be unusual simply because they would already know that children play outside in all weathers in Swedish preschools and schools. Even if your child is not used to long walks, he or she will become accustomed to them from living in Sweden; but most preschools have strollers as well and the children take turns using them. Your child won't be allowed to stay inside all day in normal circumstances, no matter what the weather.

If you mention option **Ⓓ**, you may be given a copy of the preschool curriculum, which all state preschools must follow. They are guidelines more than prescriptive though and, in general, Swedes do not like the idea of early academics for small children, even when they are aged five.

SITUATION 6

You have a good working relationship with your colleagues, and have settled into the Swedish office from the overseas headquarters well. However, you don't feel you know many of your colleagues socially and after three weeks, you'd like to meet some more of them. In the canteen one day, you sit down with an acquaintance and start a conversation. Which topic do you pick?

Ⓐ Ask your acquaintance about work—how's it going in their area? What exactly do they do? Is it very busy? and so on.

Ⓑ Comment that it's been very grey and cold lately. Does it ever get better than this? You feel quite depressed by the weather and miss the sunshine of home. When does the summer begin?

Ⓒ Mention your family and ask about your acquaintance's. Is he married? Does he have children? What are their ages?

Ⓓ Ask for her opinion about the current political situation. Can she explain the different sides to you? Which party does she think is right?

Comments

Keep in mind from the beginning that Swedes are reserved and you run the risk of alarming anyone that you approach like this. However, Swedes are generally friendly and willing to make friends—if slowly.

Option **Ⓐ** could work, although it may seem a bit like an inquisition. In general, Swedes prefer not to discuss work in their free time but as a starting topic, it is not bad.

The weather is a favourite topic in Sweden, so option **Ⓑ** is a good one. Although you should not criticise Swedes in general, criticising the weather is acceptable—Swedes do it themselves all the time. But don't overdo comments about how much better it is in your country.

Option **Ⓒ** could be perceived as a bit nosy. Swedes keep themselves to themselves until they know you better. If you want to volunteer information about your family, fine, but don't pry into theirs until you know them better.

Finally, option **❶** could be an excellent conversation starter, especially if you ask to have a specifically Swedish situation explained to you. It's not unusual to discuss politics in Sweden, but it is not usual to ask which party a Swede supports. Unlike other countries, where you can discover who a person supports through his conversation, in Sweden a political conversation will often be a general discussion of pros and cons.

Another safe topic would have been sport, particularly if Swedish teams or athletes are doing well in international competition, or new film or television. The rules governing polite conversation are the same in Sweden as elsewhere, with the proviso that Swedes are more cautious about opening up, and that you should respect their reserve.

DO'S AND DON'TS

DO'S

- Offer to take your shoes off or change to indoor shoes in private homes so that you don't track dirt, rain, or snow in. All Swedes do this.
- Bring flowers, wine or chocolates with you when you visit a Swedish home for a meal or an evening. Don't forget to remove the paper or the plastic from the flowers before you present them to your hostess.
- Remember to thank your hostess or host for the meal while still at the table, and to say *tack för senast* ('thanks for last') when you next see her or him.
- Take a number at the chemist, health centre or any other shop or office where you need to queue. Without one, you won't be served.

DON'TS

- Don't be late to a social engagement, work commitment or any appointment. Five minutes is considered rude; over 15 is unforgivable if you don't know the person you're meeting well.
- Don't criticise Sweden, even to people you are friendly with. There is an unwritten international rule that anyone is welcome to criticise their own country, but no foreigner should ever join in, particularly if they are living in the country themselves! You may not think the Swedes you are with mind, but they do.
- Don't worry about tipping—the price is generally inclusive. However, many people will round the bill up in a taxi or at an evening meal in a restaurant.

GLOSSARY

ja	yes
nej	no
hej	hello
goddag	good day
god morgon	good morning
god kväll	good evening
god natt	good night
hur mår du?	how are you?
bara bra, tack	fine, thank you
det var trevligt att träffas	it was nice to meet you
hej då	good bye
tack	thank you
tack så mycket; tusen tack	thank you so much
varsågod, varsågoda, pl	you're welcome or do go ahead (such as when holding a door or waiting) to start eating
ingen fara	no problem
snälla	please (this is not a direct translation but one can use this to mean 'please')
förlåt, förlåt mig	sorry, forgive me
ursäkta, ursäkta	excuse me
går det bra om ...	is it all right if... (literal translation is 'goes it well if..')
pratar du engelska? / talar du engelska?	do you speak English?
hjälp	help
vi ses; vi hors	see you soon; speak soon (on the phone)

RESOURCE GUIDE

Most official websites in Sweden offer at least some information in English. Look for a Union Jack flag, or a mention of 'Other Languages' if you don't see a link straight to English. Some of the links are not immediately obvious!

EMERGENCIES

The emergency numbers are 112. Use these numbers only if you need an ambulance, the police or the fire department.For a medical emergency, you can also phone your local emergency care centre (the number will be in the blue pages of the telephone directory), or go directly to your nearest hospital's casualty/accident and emergency departments.

HEALTH

When you have found a place to live, find the nearest local health care centre to register with.

HOUSING

Most of the major real estate agents are available online. For a list of current ones, you can type '*maklare*' plus your town or city into a search engine. You can also find them listed on:

http://www.gulasidorna.se.

Many Swedes rent, and you can rent for a contract of 3 months, 6 months or longer.

LANGUAGE

Your first stop should be to contact your local municipality or check on their website for adult education (*Vuxenutbilding*). You may also find information at the education website at:

http://www.skolverket.se.

There are various online options for learning, such as http://www.hhs.se/isa/swedish; and there are also many online dictionaries (including one on the skolverket website).

RELIGION

To find out more information about the Swedish Church, look at:

http://www.svenskakyrkan.se

If you need information about local places of worship in your areas, consult your local yellow pages.

GENERAL WEBSITES OF INTEREST
About Sweden

- All about Sweden, including tourist information
  http://www.sweden.se
- The Swedish Institute
  http://www.si.se
  Lots of information in English, with good links for both items of cultural interest and for students
- Study in Sweden
  http://www.studyinsweden.se

For Expatriates

- Mostly for Americans, but anyone welcome
  http://www.amerikanska.com
  Lots of useful forums and people to give advice
- More information from long term expats
  http://www.lostinsweden.com
- For parents
  www.mumsinsweden.com
  Lots of information and links to useful websites, including information on education, childcare and other topics particularly of interest to parents.

OFFICIAL WEBSITES

- Swedish statistics
  http://www.scb.se/eng
- The parliamentary website
  http://www.riksdagen.se/english
  Information about your local MP, and also about new laws.
- Immigration service
  http://www.migrationsverket.se

Downloadable applications, and clear explanations of immigration regulations.

- Swedish National Tax Board
  http://www.skatteverket.se (click on 'international' for information in English)
  Downloadable tax guide
- Social Security Office
  http://www.fk.se (click on 'other languages' for information in English)
  Lots of information about what benefits you're entitled to, but in either Swedish or simplified Swedish

Always check your own embassy's websites by typing their names and 'Sweden' or 'Stockholm' into a search engine; they may have information about clubs, groups, schools or religious organisations of interest to you.

FURTHER READING

This is a combination of the books I used myself and the books you may like to read either before or when you have moved to Sweden. They will probably help you with the transition or, at the very least, kindle some excitement in you at the thought of your move!

However, it's not easy to find books about Sweden abroad, and you may have better luck with books about Scandinavia in general. Swedish firms do publish some books in English, but these can be expensive—you can find them in any good Swedish library though.

The Swedish Institute publishes many fact sheets on different topics. You can order these by post from the Swedish Institute in Stockholm, or via their website (http://www.si.se). I have also given suggestions on Swedish literature, language books and cookery books below.

USEFUL BOOKS FOR THE TRAVELLER

Blue Guide: Sweden. Stanley Bloom. London: Blue Guides Limited, 2004 (2nd edition).
- A tourist guide specialising in the historical and artistic elements of the country.

The Rough Guide to Scandinavia. *The Rough Guides* series. 7th edition published in 2009.
- Also covers Norway, Finland and Denmark, and has an extensive section on the history of each country, as well as what to see and where to go.

The Rough Guide to Sweden. *The Rough Guides* series. 5th edition published in 2009.
- This book has more information on the culture and history of Sweden itself.

Scandinavian Europe. *Lonely Planet* series. Paul Harding etal. Victoria, Australia: Lonely Planet Publications, 2005 (7th edition).

- Sweden, Norway, Finland, Denmark, Iceland and all three Baltic nations are included. The Sweden section gives a useful overview on what to see and where to go.

Baedeker's Scandinavia, Jarrold Baedeker and Karl Baedeker. New York, NY: Prentice Hall Press, 1985.
- Covering Sweden, Norway, Denmark and Finland from a motoring tourist's perspective. Good if you plan to travel within Scandinavia on holiday.

Also Recommended

In addition, other guides, such as the *Insight Guide to Sweden*, *Fodor's Guide to Sweden* and others, offer useful advice on travelling in Sweden. The *Insight Guide* includes essays on Swedish customs, history and everyday life, intended for the traveller but useful also for the long-term visitor.

Swedish for Travellers. Lausanne, Switzerland: Berlitz Guides, 1989 (2nd edition).
- Gives commonly-used Swedish phrases, plus advice on ordering in restaurants.

USEFUL BOOKS FOR IMMIGRANTS

Sweden: a Pocket Guide. Sweden: Integrationsverket, The Swedish Integration Board, 2001.
- The official version of what you may need to know as a new immigrant to Sweden. Available free to all immigrants to Sweden; or you can download the Swedish edition from http://www.integration.se.

Modern-Day Vikings. A Practical Guide to Interacting with the Swedes. Christina Johansson Robinowitz and Lisa Werner Carr. Boston, MA: Intercultural Press, 2001.
- A wonderful book that covers the country's history and the Swedish psyche. In particular, it contains useful information on doing business with Swedes, but is aimed chiefly at Americans doing business with Swedes rather than moving to Sweden.

Living and Working in Sweden. Monica Rabe. Göteborg, Sweden: Tre Böcker Förlag, 1994.

- Looks at life in Sweden from the perspective of a Swede who has lived abroad.

Live & Work in Scandinavia. Victoria Pybus and Susan Dunne. Oxford, UK: Vacation Work Publications, 1998.

- Includes detailed information on moving to and living in Sweden, Denmark, Finland, Iceland and Norway, including many addresses. Much of the information is specific to British emigrants, but useful for others as well.

AMUSING READING
Xenophobe's Guide to the Swedes. Peter Berlin. London: Oval Books, 1999.

- A pocket-sized look at the foibles of the 'average' Swede.

Visst är det Härligt att vara Svensk! Rikard Fuchs. Stockholm, Sweden: Wahlström & Widstrand, 1991.

- For when you have learned Swedish—a Swede pokes fun at the stereotypical Swede. (The title means 'Of course it's wonderful to be Swedish!')

AVAILABLE FROM THE GOVERNMENT/ LOCAL AUTHORITIES
Sports in Sweden. Swedish Sports Confederation. Arvidsson and Yrlid (Information Sweden), 1994.

Nature in Sweden. P Hanneberg. Swedish Institute.

Swedish Forest, Skogsstyrelsen (National Board of Forestry).

HISTORY AND POLITICS
The Vikings. Johannes Brondsted. London: Penguin, 1987.

The Vikings. Else Roesdahl. London: Penguin Books Ltd, 1998.

Runes in Sweden. Sven Jansson. Sweden: Gidlunds Förlag, 1987.

The Viking burial site 'Ale Stenar' at Kaselberga.

The Gods and Myths of Northern Europe. H R David Ellison. London: Penguin Books Ltd, 1990.

Gustavus Adolphus: A History of Sweden 1611–1632. (2 vols) Michael Roberts. London: Longmans, Green & Co, 1958.

The Swedish Imperial Experience 1560–1718. Michael Roberts. Cambridge, UK: University of Cambridge, 1984.

A Concise History of Sweden. Alf Åberg. Trans. Geroge Elliott. Stockholm. Sweden: LTs Förlag, 1985.

Sweden: The Nation's History. Franklin D Scott. Carbondale, IL: Southern Illinois University Press, 1989.

Swedish Politics During the 20th Century: Conflict and Consensus, Stig Hadenius. Sweden: Swedish Institute, 1997.

A Crisis of the Welfare State?: Opinions About Taxes and Public Expenditure in Sweden. Axel Hadenius. Coronet, 1986.

A Swede dressed up as a knight during the Medieval Week festival on the island of Götaland.

The Committed Neutral: Swedish Foreign Policy. Ed. Bengt Sundelius. Boulder, CO: Westview Press Inc, 1989.
- With essays on Sweden's policy of neutrality.

FESTIVITIES AND FOOD
Majstång, Kräftor och Lucia: Svenska Festseder. Jan-Öjvind Swahn. Sweden: Swedish Institute, 1994.
- A lovely treasury of Swedish customs and holidays. Also available in English (under the name of *Maypoles, Crayfish and Lucia: Swedish Holidays and Traditions*), French and German.

Traditional Handicraft from Sweden. Svenska Hemslödsföreningen.

The Swedish Kitchen: A Culinary Journey. Lennart Hagerfors and the Swedish Culinary Team. Sweden: Norstedts Förlag, 1995.
- Includes 198 recipes from south to north featuring modern Swedish food, with commentary on their origins.

A Small Treasury of Swedish Food. The Swedish Dairies Association and The Swedish Farmers Meat Marketing Association, 1977.

Swedish Cooking. Trans. M. Sandberg and Pamela Danielsson-Theurer. Sweden: ICA Förlaget, 1998.

Pâterisserie of Scandinavia. J Audrey Ellison. New York, NY: Little Brown, 1992.

DESIGN AND ART
A History of Swedish Art. Mereth Lindgren, Louise Lyberg, Birgitta Sandström and Anna Greta Wahlberg. Lund, Sweden: Signum, 1987.

Manor Houses and Royal Castles in Sweden. Erik Liljeroth with Bengt Söderberg. Sweden: Allhems, 1975.

Quality Made in Sweden. Gunnar Hedin. Stockholm, Sweden: Informationsförlaget, 1991.

LITERATURE

An Anthology of Modern Swedish Literature. Ed. Per Wastberg. New York, NY: Merrick/Cross-Cultural Communications, 1979.

Literature in Sweden. Magnus Florin, Marianne Steinsaphir and Margareta Sörenson. Sweden: Swedish Institute, 1997.

The four *Emigrants* books (*The Emigrants*, *Unto a Good Land*, *The Settlers* and *The Last Letter Home*) by Vilhem Moberg (published by Minnesota Historical Society Press), which tell the tale of a Swedish family's emigration to America in the 19th century.

Swedish Writers

Both modern and traditional literature by Swedish authors will give you a taste of Sweden. Among the best who have been translated into English are August Strindberg, Stig Dagerman, Kerstin Ekman, Selma Lagerlöf, Sara Lidman, Agneta Pleijel, Bent Söderberg and Hjalmar Söderberg.

Reading for Children

The *Pippi Longstocking* and the *Emil* books, all by Astrid Lindgren. (There are a number of publishers of these books so check with your favourite book store.)

The Wonderful Adventures of Nils and *Further Adventures of Nils* by Selma Lagerlöf. (A popular pair of books that have been produced by different publishers. Enquire with your favourite bookseller.)

We Live In Sweden. Stephan Keeler and Chris Fairclough. London: Franklin Watts, 1985.
- A basic look at living in Sweden.

Bäckaskog castle in the town of Fjälkinge, Skane was originally built as a monastery and only converted into a fort in 1584. In the 1800s, this was the country retreat of King Karl XV. Today, the castle is a tourist attraction as well as a favourite site for conferences, weddings and other special occasions.

BUSINESS

Management and Society in Sweden. Peter Lawrence and Tony Spybey. London: Routledge & Kegan Paul, 1986.

The Swedish Economy. Barry P Bosworth. Ed. Alice M Rivlin. The Brookings Institution,1987.
- Includes essays on all aspects of Sweden's economy, including the financing of its welfare state.

'Wage Effects of Search Methods for Immigrants and Natives in Sweden'. Åsa Olli Segendorf, academic paper at Växjö University, 1998.

Staying Connected

There are many useful Internet sites about Sweden which offer information about specific topics. The Swedes have embraced the idea of the Internet and it is one of the countries with a very high percentage of users. Many Swedish Internet sites are in both Swedish and English. The country code for Sweden is '.se'

ABOUT THE AUTHOR

Charlotte Rosen Svensson grew up between cultures—with a Welsh mother and an English father—and emigrated to the United States with her family when she was a child. She went to school and college in the United States, Germany and Scotland, and decided to travel and work in Australasia after graduation.

After some time in Sydney, the outback, Hong Kong, Thailand and India and three months back in the US, she moved to London to work in publishing. After London came Sweden, in order to live with a Swede met in Bangkok and work as a language teacher; then ten more years in the UK working with international publishing. She has now returned to Sweden with her husband and children and enjoys living in a little sleepy town on the west coast.

Throughout life she hopes to continue travelling and, above all, learning about different cultures and people—and to one day finally learn how to pronounce the west coast 'sj' sound in Swedish!

INDEX

260

Titles in the CultureShock! series:

Argentina	Hawaii	Sri Lanka
Australia	Hong Kong	Shanghai
Austria	Hungary	Singapore
Bahrain	India	South Africa
Beijing	Ireland	Spain
Belgium	Italy	Sri Lanka
Berlin	Jakarta	Sweden
Bolivia	Japan	Switzerland
Borneo	Korea	Syria
Bulgaria	Laos	Taiwan
Brazil	London	Thailand
Cambodia	Malaysia	Tokyo
Canada	Mauritius	Travel Safe
Chicago	Morocco	Turkey
Chile	Munich	United Arab
China	Myanmar	Emirates
Costa Rica	Netherlands	USA
Cuba	New Zealand	Vancouver
Czech Republic	Norway	Venezuela
Denmark	Pakistan	
Ecuador	Paris	
Egypt	Philippines	
Finland	Portugal	
France	Russia	
Germany	San Francisco	
Great Britain	Saudi Arabia	
Greece	Scotland	

For more information about any of these titles, please contact any of our Marshall Cavendish offices around the world (listed on page ii) or visit our website at:

www.marshallcavendish.com/genref